Life in a
Fullness

John E. Eckersley
with
Nancy E. Eckersley

© John E. Eckersley 2020

Published by
John E. Eckersley

ISBN: 978 0 9535862 7 1

Designed and produced by
Mark Comer Design 4 Print (York)
e : comer171@yahoo.co.uk · t : 07956 612461

For Nancy
and our grandchildren:
Andrew, Beth, James, Abigail,
Lucy, Leia, Charlie, Lukas
and Natasha

ACKNOWLEDGEMENTS

This, I promise, is definitely the last book I'm writing! As with the previous walking books I've produced I have to thank numerous friends for their invaluable help and encouragement. First, I must say how grateful I am to Nancy for her patience and good humour. Apart from the few which are individually accredited, Nancy has taken all of the photos, drawn the maps, produced the cartoons and made many valuable observations. Mark Comer, who has been responsible for the design of all the other walking guides, has once again proved to be indispensable with preparing the layout of this production. Sincere thanks are again due to Liz Hassall who freely gave her time to teach Nancy her computer skills and to Phil, her husband, who has continued to be master of the website he first established for us over ten years ago.

Dan Savage, with his wonderful line drawings, and David Casson with his fine aerial photographs, provided images for some of the earlier books and I have reproduced some of those in this present publication. Again, I am most grateful for their generous involvement.

Carrie Geddes has continued to be an exceptionally efficient distributor, taking the burden of computer and paperwork from off my shoulders. Finally, I must thank my daughter Tanya, sister-in-law, Kathy, and great friend Christine Hallam for reading, checking and commenting at very short notice.

I remain indebted to you all. Thank you.

There are also three generous copyright permissions that I must acknowledge:

to *The Press* newspaper, York, for the photo on page 79

to David Harrison for the photo on page 107

and to Orion Publishers for the quotation from Jennifer Worth on page 113

Unfortunately I have been unable to trace the copyright owners for the Norman Thelwell cartoon on page 51.

Again, my thanks to you all.

The photo on the front cover was taken by Stuart and Brenda Turner and shows Nancy and myself at the end of our 1,280 miles long LEJOG Walk.

LIFE IN ALL ITS FULLNESS

CONTENTS

INTRODUCTION

Before my brother-in-law, John Siddle, died in 2015, his wife Kathy had made him write down a summary of his life. That has spurred me into doing the same and producing this little book.

Throughout my life, there have been many different passages in the Bible that I have found especially helpful but in the last few years I have been particularly impressed with a promise made by Jesus and recorded in St John's Gospel. It comes in Chapter 10, verse 10. Here Jesus says, quite simply, 'I have come so that you may have life; life in all its fullness'.

I have used this verse as the title for this book because it sums up how privileged I have been in all sorts of ways during my life as I have attempted to keep the promises that I made, when I was confirmed in 1956, to follow Jesus and to live according to his teachings.

I've been blessed, above all, with a delightful wife, four exuberant children, nine amazing grandchildren and an extended family in New Zealand as well as in this country. Add to that, I have had excellent health, a wonderful job, and enormous enjoyment running and walking for more than 60 years.

'Life in all its fullness' has nothing to do with making lots of money, or buying lots of expensive 'stuff' or becoming a famous celebrity. It is about rejoicing in the simple gifts of life. At the centre of these gifts is Love and that means knowing something about God's work in our lives.

Perhaps I should say a little about the structure of the book. My original intention was to write something like a 'Children's Story Book', especially for our grandchildren, and that's how the first few episodes may seem to read. But then I thought, 'Hang on, my life has gone on a lot longer than that and so I ought to follow through the story to its end. After all, you grandchildren will very soon grow up and may want to know what I did later on in life.' So the later episodes refer to events which, at first, might seem 'grown up' but which, hopefully, may give inspiration for you to try adventurous things later in your own lives.

I have taken the opportunity to include a few of the 'Tales' that I collected when Nancy and I were walking from Land's End to John o'Groats ('LEJOG') in 2011. They did appear at the time on our website (**www.johneckersley. wordpress.com**) but this is their first presentation in print form.

Mother and myself

EPISODE 1
Early Years

Don't be shocked, but I nearly killed my Mum some 70-odd years ago.

It was in 1942 during the Second World War and Dad was away in the army. Mum was in Park House Nursing Home in Liverpool. This was like a hospital looking after women who were sick or about to have babies. Apparently, I learned many years later, I was a very difficult birth. My Mum became unconscious and when she came round the first words she heard the doctor speak were to the waiting nurse: 'You can take that trolley back to the mortuary; the mother is going to live after all'. They had really expected my Mum to die, but no, she had survived. Perhaps that experience helps to explain the amazing love mothers have for their children.

As Dad was away in the War, it was Mum who looked after me for my first three years but, to make sure I knew what my Dad looked like, I was given a photo of him which I kept in my shirt pocket. When Dad at last did come home and Mum said to me 'Here's your Daddy, John' I didn't believe her. 'No', I cried, 'that's not my Daddy; **here's** my Daddy!' and I pulled out his photo from my pocket.

Dad

Life was hard for my Mum and Dad after the War, although, because I had never known anything different, I just assumed it was normal. My sister Maureen was born four years after me and during the dreadful winter of 1946-47 it was difficult to care for a young baby. We moved from 35 Sandringham Road (Liverpool 22) to 30 Tuscan Street (Liverpool 21).

9

Here there was no electricity; only one (very slow flowing) cold water tap and, of course, no inside toilet and no bath. The toilet was outside in the back yard and when we needed a bath, Mum had to boil pans of water and then carry them to the tin bath in the living room.

After a few years we got the great news that we had been given a council house in nearby Thornton. We were over the moon. A council house – with **six** taps (including three hot water ones), a bath, a toilet, electricity, a room each for Maureen and myself, a small garden and a view out across green playing fields. It sounded like paradise.

When I was five, I had started at **Crosby Road North Primary School**. For my first two years I had a wonderful teacher, Miss Ellison. Then later, in the top junior class, I played for the school football team.

Me at Junior School

As with many lads of my age, I was mad on football. The following Tale from my sister Maureen, which first appeared on our website when we were walking LEJOG, gives a flavour of the fervour.

A Kiwi Tale by Maureen Evason (née Eckersley)

Hello. I'm John's sister and I have been living in New Zealand with my husband Bill for about 37 years.

John has persuaded me to write a tale from 'down under' and so I thought that I would tell you a couple of things about John that you may not know.

We were born and raised in Liverpool. John has always been the older and wiser(?) sibling. He is kind and considerate and can become incredibly enthusiastic about new adventures...such as LEJOG.

When we were young, John was introduced to the game of Monopoly. He was very keen, but could not afford to buy his own game. Undeterred, he spent hours and hours meticulously cutting, writing and colouring all those little cards and banknotes. He made the big board too. Guess who was press-ganged into playing at home? He didn't even let me win! Such was his enthusiasm!

Several years later came his 'running years'. He would put on his trainers and don his little blue shorts with the white stripes down the sides, leave the house, slamming the front door behind him (amazingly only shattering the glass in it twice) and proceed to jog around the streets of our neighbourhood. This was in the days when **nobody** else did this but John was oblivious to the astonished stares of people he passed. He was going to keep fit! To my mortification this regime lasted for some considerable time.

As you may know, Liverpool has many good footballers and there has always been great rivalry between its two teams, Liverpool and Everton.

One day John came home from school and, making his first attempt at teenage rebellion (even though he was only 11) proclaimed to our father, a staunch Liverpool supporter, 'Dad, I've seen the light! I've been converted! Liverpool is not the best football team – Everton is!' He'd been given this revelation by his pal, David, who was captain of the school team.

From that day onwards ours was a divided household, never to see the solidarity and unity that an all-Red or all-Blue family might expect to share. No mature counselling or fatherly advice would ever persuade my brother that he had been misled.

So John grew up a loyal, enthusiastic fan of The Blues. I remember all too well his deafening football 'rattle' that he would practise twirling at home (until it was banned from inside the house); the blue and white rosette (he still has it, treasured in its special box) and the blue bob hat Mum knitted specially for him (Nancy inadvertently lost this bit of dog-eared memorabilia). He was, and still is, an ardent Evertonian.

Naturally, my Dad and brother did not go to watch football together, but there was one occasion when they did. It was a Liverpool-Everton derby game at Anfield, Liverpool's ground. Somehow Dad had managed to get two tickets for the Kop (the Liverpool supporters' end of the ground) and he and John stood together on the packed terraces. What a game! Everton (Blue) trounced Liverpool (Red) 4-0; but John, the only Blues' supporter standing amongst literally thousands of Reds' fans, did not dare to utter even a whisper of a cheer! Yet John tells me that after the game, Dad was the epitome of the good sportsman, without a grudge or excuse or word of malice. It was all incredibly good-humoured.

Years later John, married with four young children and living in York, took his three eldest to a local FA cup game. York City had been drawn to play at home to Everton. A decade earlier York had played Liverpool in the FA Cup two years running and John, of course, had been delighted to join his children and enthuse about the possibility of York beating The Reds! Now came a much sterner test. Would John be able to emulate our father's behaviour from years ago? He tells me, and I must believe him, that he went genuinely intending to remain neutral. However, after the first ten minutes he couldn't stop himself...he was supporting his old favourites, Everton (who subsequently lost 3-2 in what was a cracking game, points out one of John's sons). Later he admitted how surprised he had been at his old deep-rooted allegiance.

I hope that I've been able to give you a glimmer of my brother's almost life-long enthusiasm for Everton FC. When he and Nancy were planning their long LEJOG walk, I offered him a challenge that I knew he would not like doing! If he wore a Liverpool hat and shirt, not covered by a mac or jacket or the Christian Aid tabard for a whole day, then I would sponsor him for the LEJOG walk. I was confident that John was enthusiastic enough about Christian Aid to take up the challenge and I'm delighted that he did.

Christ Church was very important for me as I grew up. I learned the Christian story from my Mother but there was also a number of kind teachers in the Church. And as well, there was a great Scout Group. I owe the Scouts an enormous amount for all they taught me.

It was the Scouts that gave me a love of nature and the outdoors, taught me to swim and gave me the chance to go on cheap camping holidays at a time when our family could not afford to go away.

The Scouts introduced me to walking and when I was 17, I went with two other lads to the Lake District on a three day, 47 mile hike carrying all our kit. On Day Two we came to Great Langdale and I fell in love with the place immediately.

Great Langdale

Years later, I would go to Langdale regularly on school field trips and it never lost its magic. In fact, at a church meeting years later, we were discussing what Heaven might be like and we were asked for our ideas of the celestial realm. I had no hesitation in declaring that my ideal would be to walk and run among the hills and valleys of Langdale (assuming, of course, it doesn't sile down with rain in Heaven).

Above all, the Scouts was great fun! When I was only 14, I had the privilege of being unofficial Scoutmaster for three weeks. 'Mac', the real leader, had had to move on and the Group Scoutmaster, George Fraser, agreed that I should stand in and do the job for a few weeks until a 'real' replacement came to take it on. Three weeks later, Jeff Roberts came back from doing his National Service and immediately took on the role of Scoutmaster. More than sixty years later, Jeff is still actively involved with Scouting – an exceptional example of dedicated voluntary public service.

I also had a very enjoyable time at **Waterloo Grammar School (WGS)**. School is a time when we start having to make important decisions about our future lives, so we need to think very carefully about them. Let me tell you about some of those decisions I had to make.

Perhaps the first was to decide whether or not I wanted to get confirmed. Confirmation in the Church is the time when people say 'Yes, I believe in Jesus and I want to spend my life following him and his ideas'. I did want to follow Jesus and so I got confirmed when I was 13.

Later on, I thought that I might become a teacher. But should I teach big children or little ones; what subject should I teach; where should I go to study; where should I actually teach? All these questions went through my mind as I tried to decide what to do. Eventually, I decided that I would like to teach Geography and PE at Secondary School level. I am glad to say that's what eventually happened. Whew!

After two years in the **Sixth Form** I applied for University. But I was not accepted by any of my three choices. Naturally, I was disappointed and had to decide what to do next. Fortunately, I wasn't the only one of my class who had failed to get a University place and we were encouraged to stay for another year in the Sixth Form and then to apply again. That's what I did. And it turned out to be one of the best things that ever happened to me. I say this because the third year in the Sixth Form was the time when I really improved in confidence (and ability) in the subjects I was studying and so when I did go to University I was far better prepared than I would have been if I had gone the year earlier. The lesson I learned from that experience was that sometimes in life we have to wait and not rush into doing things too quickly. It's a lesson I've found hard to learn and Nancy is still often having to tell me to be patient and wait until the time is right.

Athletics at WGS

Staying on an extra year at WGS also gave me the opportunity to spend more time doing sport. I had already been in the School teams for football and athletics but in my last year I was made captain for both.

Every so often, the footballers played a game against the staff; very generous of the teachers, we agreed, but it was not a walk-over for us students. I remember one occasion when I went down in a vigorous tackle and was writhing on the ground I overheard (though I'm sure I wasn't meant to) Nye Williams, our charismatic History teacher, mutter, 'What amazes me is that he doesn't get more injuries, the way he plays!' I took this as a compliment, implying that I played my game with a fair deal of enthusiasm.

However, on another occasion, I badly strained a thigh muscle and this meant that I could not raise my foot to kick a ball without aggravating the injury. On the other hand, when I was running with a steady rhythm, there was no problem and that's how running overtook football as my main sport and remained so for the next 50 years or so.

John Crompton, who was a great friend at WGS and who managed to excel at every different sport he tried, was also finding athletics becoming increasingly pre-eminent. On the track we were both keen 400 metre (440 yards in those days) runners but such middle distance runners were two a penny. Somehow, and I can't remember what it was, we both decided that we would stand a better chance of getting team places if we switched from 'flat' 400 metre races to 400 metre hurdling instead. That's what we both did when John went to Loughborough and I went to Durham.

EPISODE 2
Student Years

I started at **Durham University** in October 1962 and one of the first things I had to learn was how to survive between 5.00 o'clock (the time at home when we had always had our evening 'Tea') and 7.00 o'clock which was the time they served 'Dinner' at Uni. It took me a few weeks to realise that most students just added another meal –'afternoon tea' – into their normal routine. After that, all was fine.

By and large I enjoyed the Geography (although I found map projections were diabolical) and we had some inspiring lecturers. One of the most memorable times at University was the 'Field Trip' we went on to the Rhine Valley in Germany which included a tour of the West German Parliament in Bonn.

It was the first time I had ever been abroad and it was an eye-opening experience for me. I have to record that there was a minimum amount of 'field work' carried out but we all, needless to say, had a whale of a time. (And don't forget, this was all part of our studies, so was paid for by the state.) We had one entirely free day and I hitched down the Rhine. It was spring time and the famous cherry blossoms looked magnificent in the sunshine. Lifts came readily and I knew that this had been a very special day.

I was pleased that the sporting opportunities were so good at Durham. I mentioned in the last episode how at school I had sustained an injury which made kicking a football difficult but my running was not affected. This meant I concentrated on cross-country and hurdling while I was at Durham. Each of the colleges had its own sports teams, so even if you were not good enough to play for the University teams, there were plenty of opportunities to represent your college.

One of my friends was a student called Chris and, like me, he was a keen Everton supporter. In 1963 Everton had won the English League title (what today would be the Premiership) and Glasgow Rangers had been champions of the Scottish League. It was the tradition for the English and Scottish champions to play against each other for the British Championship title, so Rangers were playing Everton at Ibrox Park in Glasgow. Chris suggested that we could hitch-hike up to Scotland to see the game. It sounded mad, but Chris managed to persuade me that it was a good idea.

We set off early on the morning of the game, hitched lifts up the A1 from Durham, through Newcastle and Berwick and on to Edinburgh. So far, so good. However, we thought it would be sensible to take a train from Edinburgh across central Scotland to Glasgow and so that's what we did. Timing was perfect; we arrived at Ibrox at 7.25pm and the kick-off was at 7.30pm – we couldn't believe our good fortune.

Before we had started the journey Chris had suggested that we should wear College scarves because that would help us to get lifts more easily – motorists might be more sympathetic towards poor, penniless students. My problem was that I didn't have a College scarf. However, my house-mate Tony did have one and he kindly offered to loan me his. I think it probably did help us because we managed extremely well to get lifts.

But there was one big problem. Our College scarves were green and white; and green and white were the colours of Glasgow Celtic who, as most people know, are Rangers bitter rivals. I had totally forgotten this minor detail until someone inside the ground asked me why we were sporting green and white at Rangers. Horrified we realised our dreadful mistake and, quick as a flash, whipped off the offending garments and stuffed them inside our duffle coats. 64,000 whisky-swigging, difficult-to-understand Glaswegians might not, we thought, be very sympathetic towards two foolish Englishmen.

To be honest, I had forgotten what the score of the game had been and I had to ask our son Peter to check it on the internet for me. For the record, though, Everton won 3-1 and then later, because it was a two-leg competition, drew the second leg 1-1 at Goodison, thus becoming British Champions. Happy days.

Anyway, by 9.15 all the excitement was over and we had to face the prospect of getting home. We raced back to the railway station and, just as its doors were closing, jumped on the train back to Edinburgh. From there, it was about 140 miles hitching through the night down the A1 to Durham.

I don't recall all the lifts we were fortunate to get but I do remember that early on a police patrol van stopped and the cops asked us what we were up to. So we waved our scarves for them. They obviously liked our story, felt sorry for us and gave us a lift to the end of their patrol patch.

A lift in an early morning bread delivery van came at some stage and then, as it was getting light, we managed to reach Newcastle. From there we caught the early bus for the last 20 miles or so to Durham. Feeling pretty pleased with myself, I rolled into my 9.00 o'clock lecture bang on time. 'Street cred' hadn't been invented in those days but if it had been, I reckon mine would have jumped high up the graph.

'You must have been mad.' Well, yes, that's probably true. But there again that's the sort of crazy thing students did in those days. And today? I don't imagine things have greatly changed.

Loughborough

As I said earlier, I had already decided when I was at school that I wanted to teach. However, I realised that I would need to have, in addition to a degree, a teaching certificate or Postgraduate Certificate in Education (PGCE). John Crompton encouraged me to apply to Loughborough College to do this course – there was a special one year Graduate course as well as the normal three year Certificate, which John was already studying. I was hesitant – Loughborough had a fairly substantial claim to be the foremost PE College in the country and I doubted whether my abilities would match up. Nevertheless, I applied and to my great satisfaction was accepted. One of the advantages of the Loughborough course was that, in addition to the Loughborough Diploma, you also got a PGCE Certificate from Nottingham University.

I shared a room with John at Quorn, one of the college halls, and had the dubious pleasure of being lulled to sleep every Saturday night by Jones the Shot Put. Every week he would gently roll a 16 pounder cannon ball down the wooden stairs, step by step, thud by thud, right down to the bottom and then repeat the 'training exercise' all over again. It brought back memories of my last year at Durham when I had been treated to a similar display of athletic perseverance when two guys in our hall would chase each other up and down the stairs practising their sword fencing skills – it's surprising what a racket two thin bits of steel can create when they clash against each other.

There was a distinct feeling that Loughborough, a college, was trying to improve its academic credentials by having a graduate course and in order to do that, it needed to justify itself by claiming that PE was not just about playing games but was designed 'to inculcate a feeling of well-being'. There were 24 Grads in our year's intake and they all thought this was hilarious and it soon became clear that we were all there mainly for a year's fun and games. It was great – playing footie and running, all paid for by the state. But it could be tough.

On the staff was Robbie Brightwell who, the year before, had been Captain of the British Athletics team at the 1964 Tokyo Olympics and had won a silver medal in the 4x400 metres relay. He organised punishing training sessions in the nearby Charnwood Hills and I can still hear him telling us after each time out, 'That was a gooood session, lads; a gooood session.' We certainly felt we had been put through our paces.

As well as doing PE we had to gain a qualification in the subject that we had studied previously at University which was, in my case, Geography. There were four of us Geographers and the tutor kindly invited us round to his house for a meal one evening. After eating, he told us that he was going to teach us to play Scrabble. We couldn't believe it; England were playing on the box that night and we, naturally, wanted to watch the game. We argued but he was having none of it – we had to learn to play Scrabble! It seemed to us an amazing example of insensitivity. It would be some years before I ever considered playing the game again.

It had been a great year and I now started preparing for the next stage of my life.

VSO in Sudan

The first teaching job I had was in the Sudan in Africa. At the time it was the biggest country in Africa.

For some time I had had the idea of doing some sort of overseas voluntary work – the sort of thing that is nowadays called a 'gap year'. I felt that I had been so richly blessed in all the good things that I had enjoyed so far in my life that I wanted to try to give just a little bit back to help some of the world's poorer people. So I applied to go on VSO ('Voluntary Service Overseas'). At the interview, in a cold London office, I was asked where I would like to go. 'Somewhere hot,' I said. Shortly afterwards I got a reply: 'We're sending you to Dongola in the Sudan; July temperature is 104 degrees Fahrenheit (that's 40 Celsius!)'. 'What!' I thought, 'someone's got a sense of humour'.

As it happened, when I arrived in Sudan I was sent, not to Dongola, but to a place called Gedaref. This was a town where the **students** had recently gone on strike because they wanted more teachers. Just imagine what might happen if the older students at our schools went on a demonstration demanding more teachers.

Local dress – djellaba and turban

18

The students I was teaching were at the equivalent stage of English 'O' (or GCSE) level. A good number of their subjects were still being taught in English, although Arabic and RE (Islam) were understandably in Arabic. Some of them were studying English Literature as well as English Language and I marvelled at their facility to understand Shakespeare in a foreign tongue.

As well as teaching them 'Macbeth', I had the delight of trying to help them understand the complexities of Oscar Wilde's 'The Importance of Being Earnest'. You may recall that one of the key elements of Wilde's comedy is the play on words between 'Earnest' (meaning serious) and 'Ernest' (used as a man's name). My difficulties were somewhat alleviated by the fact that I could tell them that my middle name, taken after my Dad, was 'Ernest'.

At this point in my life story maybe I should say how being called 'Ernest' (spelt without an 'a') has been the cause of a fair bit of jocularity in our family because, nowadays, it's not a common name. The four children have taken every opportunity to tease me (egged on, of course, by my adoring wife) and whenever we sing the hymn about 'The Journey of Life....' I am fully aware of the vibes coming from her direction as she sings this song with even greater gusto than usual. Our daughter Tanya even made the suggestion that I could call this book 'My J'Ernie of Life'. And it goes further than that. Someone (you'll never guess who) thought the title for my mini-biography might more properly be 'A Thanksgiving Jernal'.

I stayed for two happy years in the Sudan and was treated with extraordinary kindness by the staff and local people. The following story illustrates what I mean. Where I was in the Sudan there is a big difference between the wet season and the dry season. In the wet, travel is difficult because most of the roads are dirt or mud roads without a hard tarmac surface and so are often impassable. I wanted to go to Khartoum, the capital city, and the rainy season had just about come to an end so travel should have been all right. But there were no buses doing the journey so instead I used the normal method and hitched a lift on the back of a lorry.

We got to Khartoum safely but on the way back there was a problem – in fact, a major problem. We got stuck in the mud at a point in the journey where the ground was still wet after the rains. The driver and his mates tried all sorts of tricks to get out of the mud but things seemed to get even worse – and it was now dark! What could we do?

Well, something rather amazing happened. Out of the dark a young man called Mohamed came forward. 'Hello, Mr John,' he said 'I can help you.' Mohamed, in fact, was one of my students from school. **Somehow**, he had learned that I had been going to Khartoum; that I would be coming back through his village; that I would be on the back of a lorry; and that the lorry might just get stuck. And having learned all this, he had gone to the trouble of preparing a welcome for me, just in case the lorry got stuck. 'Here's your bed, Mr John', said Mohamed as he led me to a bed already laid out under the stars just for me. I was speechless, apart, that is from saying, several times 'Shukran, shukran jezeelan!' 'Thank you, thank you so much!' Over the years, I have often thought of this wonderfully generous act of hospitality. I wish more people in our country would show this kind of friendship to visitors from other countries.

Climbing Kilimanjaro

Another very memorable event of my time in Africa was going to tour some of the East African Game Parks during the long summer break between the two years I was in Sudan. The highlight of the holiday, though, was climbing Kilimanjaro, Africa's highest peak at 19,340 feet. Three of us VSOs, Graham Darby, Andrew Stone and myself took up the challenge.

The climbing club in Nairobi were extremely generous in kitting us out with all the necessary gear including warm clothes, boots and snow goggles. There was a well-established routine. You took three days to climb up the mountain and two days to come down. Accommodation was in wooden huts along the way. It was the final steep climb that was the really testing part. The guides got us out of bed (actually we had hardly slept) well before sunrise and we started off. As the air got thinner I remember having to rest and lean on my climbing stick every three or four paces to get my breath back. We struggled

Gilman's Point, Kilimanjaro, except the snow line was some 3,000 feet lower in 1967

on. It was snow and ice all the way to the top. Yet as the photo shows, there has since been a catastrophic reduction in the amount left, caused, of course, by global warming.

Kilimanjaro has three volcanic cones: Kibo, Mawenzi and Shira, and it was Kibo, the highest, which we were climbing. There are two recognised 'summits'. The first is Gilman's Point which is on the crater rim at the top of the slope we were ascending. A little further around the rim is Uhuru Peak which is higher. We could only get to Gilman's Point because the guides said the conditions were too severe to go any further. But we were still justified in claiming we had climbed Kilimanjaro.

Why did I come back to England from Sudan? The main reason was that I wanted to find a wife. When I tried to explain this to my class (they all wanted me to stay) some of them immediately cried out 'Oh, Mr John, that's no problem; I've got a sister you can have for a wife!' And they were serious.

I travelled home to England with Graham Darby, first taking the train across the Sahara Desert to the Aswan High Dam in Egypt and then visiting some of the main historical sites along the Nile Valley. When I arrived back in England, I found that Everton would soon be playing in the FA Cup Final at Wembley. I had never been to Wembley before and somehow my pal Brian managed to buy me a ticket for the game. Four of us met on the steps of the ground, had a great reunion but unfortunately saw the Blues get beaten.

EPISODE 3
Manchester and Early York

Back in England, I managed to get a job teaching Geography and PE at Stand Grammar School for Boys in Whitefield, north Manchester. At Stand there was plenty of opportunity for continuing with my own sport, although by this time I had concentrated on hurdling and cross country, with football as an extra.

On the staff the Latin teacher was a man called **Dennis Weir**. Dennis and his wife Margaret became long-standing friends. As well as holding a string of records for fell walks, Dennis had an outstanding record as an 'ultra' distance runner. He held ultra-distance Over-50s World Track records for 30 miles, 100 miles, 50 km, 100 km, 200 km and 12 hours. I felt honoured to be in his company.

The other thing about Dennis is that he was, and still is, a very good fell runner and he introduced me to this sort of running. The 'fells' is another name for 'hills' and 'fell running' means running up and down hills and mountains. I was immediately hooked – it combined my love for hill walking with that for traditional cross-country running. And it had the extra attraction that it was a special kind of running that not many people took part in. Some people couldn't understand why I wanted to **run** up **mountains** but that made it all the more exciting.

One of the highlights of the fell-runners' calendar is the Yorkshire Three Peaks Race that includes running up Ingleborough, Pen-y-Ghent and Whernside in the Yorkshire Dales. For my first attempt at the race, Dennis advised me to try to follow the legendary Stan Bradshaw. (Dennis alludes to Stan in his Tale below.) I ran the Three Peaks race for several years but never managed to break the magical 3-hour barrier.

Whilst I was at Stand, Dennis told me that he was going to attempt to break the record for running the recently opened 268 mile long Pennine Way, the first of the country's National Trails. Would I be interested in acting as support for him? I jumped at the chance, although there was one problem: I was planning to try to run the route myself with a contact I had made when at Loughborough, Alistair Lawson, and our dates would overlap with those of Dennis. In the end, I decided that Alistair and I would only be able to complete the southern section of the PW and I would act as Dennis' support. That's what happened.

Al and I had a great time on our run but he was noticeably faster than me. Accordingly, I devised a set of ruses to slow him down. I would make just a short sprint to the next gate or stile, get there first and then take an inordinate length of time to negotiate the hurdle. Or, I seemed to have terribly loose shoe laces that required constant adjustment; or, I insisted on stopping to check the map to ensure Al's navigation was correct. Astonishingly, it took Al quite a time to see through my tricks. But we never did finish the last northern part of the Pennine Way and I still get reminders from him, 50 years on, that we ought to complete it at some time.

The P.W. Runner's Tale by Dennis Weir

John and I were colleagues at Stand Grammar School in Manchester. He had a reputation for being an accident zone: handles would mysteriously break off hot mugs of tea when he picked them up; notice boards would suddenly fall from their perches when he walked past; and on the very first day that he drove his car to work he hit the school wall. But it was as part time PE teachers actively involved in athletics that we shared a common interest. He was a 440 yards hurdler while I was into long-distance running. Together we organised a Track and Field League for Manchester Schools and started running together on the Peak District Moors.

Eventually John felt strong enough to enter his first Fell Race – the iconic Yorkshire Three Peaks of Ingleborough, Whernside and Pen-y-Ghent. Not too many hurdlers enter the Three Peaks, so to avoid too fast a start, I suggested that John find and follow the legendary fell-runner Stan Bradshaw and this would guarantee an award-winning time. 'But beware,' I warned, 'if Stan feels he is being taken for granted, he'll stop and pretend he has to tie his shoelace. While you carry on, he'll disappear into the mist.' John followed my advice but during the race, Stan really did twist his ankle and had to stop. 'You can't fool me, Stan,' quipped John merrily, 'I've heard all about your little tricks.' Even the saintly Stan showed signs of irritation but in due course he led John to the finish and to a creditable time.

On one occasion we took a party of 'O' Level lads on a walking / running / history / Latin trip to Hadrian's Wall in Northumbria. One night I lay, tossing and turning in my Youth Hostel bunk, kept awake in this idyllic countryside by the wailing of a Bellingham disco. John was sound asleep. Suddenly I recalled that an attempt on the Pennine Way relay record was shortly due to pass through the village and – flash! Why don't I run it end-to-end? In the morning, John unhesitatingly agreed to help. It meant that he would have to curtail his own Pennine Way run that he was planning with Alistair Lawson but he was willing to sacrifice that in order to act as my support.

The individual record stood at just over seven days and so in 1970 with Ted Dance, a friend from the Rucksack Club, I decided to aim for five days. John did all the driving for us and with my wife Margaret and our five year-old son Robert, fed us, patched blisters, read fairy stories, sang umpteen nursery rhymes and gave cheerful encouragement at every stop. We stayed at Youth Hostels, which we had vetted first so that fierce wardens (a lot of them in those days) were avoided. Of course John being John, there had to be a minor glitch. After the longest drive of the whole trail, it was discovered that the bag of clean socks had been left behind. So John had to do the double journey again. He still met us on schedule and only told us afterwards that he'd also found time to land the car in a ditch on that same leg of the journey. (Surely he'd not fallen asleep?!)

The last hostel was Earby where the warden sacrificed his own supply of hot water so that Ted and I could soak in a bath. All the bunks sloped sideways and so we had to hold ourselves in to stop rolling on to the floor. John, of course, slept soundly.

After that, Stan Bradshaw met us on the Peak District moors with a flask of hot soup and offered to keep us company for a couple of hours. In fact, he stayed with us through the rest of the day and the following night and delivered us safely to John at Edale. We finished on 10th August, my wedding anniversary, beating the five day barrier by just 40 minutes. We'd smashed

I owe Dennis and Margaret an enormous debt for introducing me to fell-running and the adventure Dennis has just described did, indeed, develop my appetite for long-distance trailing.

the record! Stan had been a great help but without John the record just would not have been possible.

The modern individual record for running the Pennine Way is less than three days. The holder made do with just one hour of sleep in the entire journey. Nevertheless I like to think that our venture sowed the seed in John's mind for the sort of mighty epic that he and Nancy undertook in completing LEJOG.

Oh, I nearly forgot. I was high on adrenalin and feeling remarkably perky after running 268 miles in five days and setting a new long distance record, so naturally, I drove us all home. John took a well-earned nap in the passenger seat.

I was in my late twenties when I was running in Manchester and before then it was generally thought that most sportspeople would have given up their game before they were 40 or so. Anyone who did compete after 40 was classed as a Veteran and I had secret hopes that, one year, I would enter that category. Apart from anything else, there would be so few competitors in the group that I might stand a chance of getting a place! As it turned out, although I was not racing competitively, I was still running regularly until I was 68 and only stopped because, after five months walking Land's End to John o'Groats, I couldn't get back into the rhythm. I still find it astonishing that the great running boom encouraged by celebrities such as Brendan Foster and Chris Brasher has maintained its momentum and, with the advent of Park Runs, has become even more popular.

There are no prizes for guessing who the other very important person was that I met in north Manchester. Meeting **Nancy** happened like this. When I took accommodation in Prestwich, the suburb next to Whitefield, I attached myself to St Margaret's which was the local church; in fact it was the church where my head of department played the organ. Shortly after arriving, the curate, Simon, was preaching and announced that he would soon be leaving and wondered if there was there anyone in the church who might be willing to become the Youth Fellowship leader when he left. The request hit me like the proverbial bolt from the blue.

I've since realised that one of the signs that God is speaking to us is that he often says things that are completely and totally unexpected. But the Inner Voice, the Holy Spirit, the conviction or whatever name you choose to describe God, is so unexpected and clear that it cannot be just our own imagining. What was especially interesting for me was that I had thought that, after teaching in Sudan, I could offer to teach English as a second language to people in Manchester. I tried a couple of times to see if this was possible but there was no opening available. Offering to take on the Youth Fellowship therefore seemed to be God's directing.

Most of the Youth Fellowship group at St Margaret's were shortly going to leave to go to university, so I would be inheriting a new set of faces. But before that, I was introduced to the older group. Apparently, I did not make much of an impression. I did, however, make the acquaintance of a certain Miss Nancy Carter who was one of those about to start University in a couple of months' time.

At Easter, two terms later, Miss Carter returned to St Margaret's and at coffee after the service, we happened to chat about holiday plans. We found that we would both be going to France that summer, for entirely different types of holiday, but we would be in Paris on the same day. 'How about meeting up at the north-west corner of the Eiffel Tower?' I said jokingly. And so the date was made. I'll tell you my side of the story now. (But then you may want to read Nancy's account to see if she remembers it differently.)

My version

You will remember that I said earlier that during the Second World War, my Dad had been away in foreign lands so he knew a little of what it was like to live abroad in a different country. Mother (now that I was older, she said that she preferred to be called that rather than 'Mum') on the other hand had never been abroad, so that summer I had taken her for a short holiday to the Mediterranean coast in southern France. It was great and she felt good that she had had the courage to go overseas.

On the way down to the Mediterranean, we were staying in Versailles, some distance away from Paris but I kept remembering that I had made a sort of joking date with a young student from Manchester called Nancy Carter. But it was a long way to get to the Eiffel Tower; surely she would realise that it had all just been a joke, I said to myself. What if I make the journey and she's not there? It will have been a complete waste of time. There are thousands of people at the Eiffel Tower every day, so how will I find her among all the crowds?

But somehow a nagging thought at the back of my mind kept saying; 'Yes, you ought to go; she'll be expecting you.' I had to make a decision. Should I go or not? You have probably guessed that I decided to follow my instinct (by now you'll have understood that, for me, my 'instinct' usually meant the same thing as God's Voice or God's Spirit guiding me what to do).

So I went. And, would you believe it, there's no such place as 'the north-west corner of the Eiffel Tower' so my Mother and I had to walk around the bottom of the Tower hoping to find Miss Carter. Then, lo and behold, there she was with her student friend Lynn. I have to say, I expected them to be looking tired and pretty miserable because I was late. But no; instead I was greeted with huge smiles. 'Mmmmm,' I thought, 'I wonder why she's waited so long for me ...?' I soon found out.

'You've come at long last!' she cried. 'We've run out of money, we've run out of food and it's still a long way back to England!'

So there I was, the gallant knight in bright shining armour, coming to rescue the two fair damsels in distress. They scoffed all my spare food (especially the bananas, if I remember rightly) borrowed some money (you have to pay to go to the toilets in Paris) and even persuaded me to pay for them to go up the Eiffel Tower.

However, climbing up the Tower took us longer than expected and because Mother had decided to wait for us at the bottom, it meant that she had a very long wait before we finally came down. I felt guilty that I had left her so long in a strange country, not speaking any French but she never complained. I wonder: did she suspect that Nancy had been chatting me up all that time?

Nancy's version

Lynn and I had been in France for six weeks working part of the time for a German woman, Hanna, on her building site in the Massif Central and part of the time hitching round the South of France sight-seeing. At the end of the six weeks all we had left were our train and ferry tickets home but no money. Hanna gave us a lift to the overnight train in Nimes and we managed to cadge breakfast from an American tourist on the Gare de Lyon station. Our train north to Calais was not due until six in the evening. We had no food and not even enough to pay to go to the toilets! 'I know' I said, 'there is a chance that this guy John might turn up at the Eiffel Tower (NW corner) at 12 noon. It's worth a try.' So we walked through Paris, with the American guy, who obviously fancied Lynn, tagging along. We had plenty of time but no money to do anything. When we got to the Tower, we found to our dismay that there wasn't a NW corner so we spent the rest of the time walking between the north and west corners until - yes - lunch, and even tickets up the Tower and, most importantly, centimes pour les toilettes! came into view in the shape of John and his mum.

We made our separate ways, Mother and I in our Mini car to explore France and Nancy and Lynn back to Manchester.

Soon after, Nancy and I met, quite by chance, in the local launderette in Prestwich. I was doing the washing after my trip to France and Nancy, who just happened to be passing by, spotted me, came in and stopped for a brief chat. Later that week I rang her and asked her if she would like to go to a party with me. To my surprise, she agreed. She came but sadly got drunk and was sick. Nancy must have thought that she had got rid of me by now but no – I asked her out again. I had joined the Manchester Film Society, a sort of semi-highbrow club that specialised in showing films for which there was only a limited market. I asked Nancy if she fancied coming to see 'The Mad Woman of Chaillot' with me, which, although it might have been important in the development of cinematography, I have to admit we both thought was dreadful and we left part way through. I then took her to another party, which was equally as dire as the first one had been, and then to a second film (Doctor Zhivago) which, unbeknown to me, she had seen before and knew she would like. Later that month I asked if I could write to her when she returned to University in a few days' time. She said 'Yes' and from then on we started corresponding with each other. Cutting a short story even shorter, three months later, on 6th December 1970, we decided that we wanted to get married and so we became engaged.

We didn't tell Nancy's parents then but when we did, they, to put it very mildly, expressed their astonishment. Her brother Pete was equally distraught – he was in one of my Geography classes at Stand!

For a number of years I had been praying for a Christian wife. Finding Nancy had all started with my answering God's call to take on the Church Youth Fellowship Group. If I had not done that, I probably would not have met her. And not only did God send me a wife who would become a Christian, but he sent me someone who would become a Vicar! God sometimes gives us far more than we ask – so be careful what you pray for!

There are two little cameos that I should tell you about before we moved to York.

One weekend Nancy and I visited my sister Maureen in Shipley. Unfortunately there was a power cut and so we had only candles and firelight to see by. Mo suggested that we played **Scrabble** – my heart sank with dreadful memories of the one and only time I had played it while at Loughborough. 'Oh, come on, John,' said Mo, 'you'll enjoy it this time.' And so we did; in fact both Nancy and I became hooked. Wait for later in this Episode to hear the next stage of the Scrabble saga.

The other tale relates to the noble social service of **blood donating**. We had been shopping in Manchester and Nancy, who had been a blood donor for several years, noticed the blood donor centre in town and suggested we went in and gave blood. I thought it my civic duty to join the ranks and offered to become a donor there and then for the first time. The nurse told me that the only painful bit was the jab in the thumb to test whether my blood was suitable or not. I survived this without the slightest hint of a flinch and so was then asked to lie down. Nancy's blood was taken first and then it was my turn. The needle went in, and the tube filled up with first class A Positive stuff. I then made the foolish move of glancing sideways, seeing what was happening and immediately freaked out. 'Nuuuuurse!' I groaned. Said nurse immediately hurried over, undid the tube, raised the bed and plied me a big cup of sugary tea. 'Thank you ever so much Mr Eckersley but I don't really think you should become a blood donor' she said. So much for my public spirited sacrifice.

Nurse then arranged for me to be taken home in a taxi as soon as I felt fit enough. Nancy, however, received no such kindly attention. She was left to catch a bus and make her own way back to Prestwich, carrying all our shopping with her. How unfair can you get! What remains a puzzle all these years later is why neither of us had the presence of mind to question why Nancy could not come back with me in the taxi. I have since learned that the name for fear of needles is 'needle phobia'.

Early Years in York

At that time I had been teaching for nearly three years in Manchester and it was time for me to move on. I applied for a job teaching at Queen Anne Grammar School for Girls in York because Nancy was studying Biology at York University. 'And why are you wanting to come to York?' asked Irene Whittaker, the headmistress, at my interview. 'Well, my girl-friend is a student in York,' I said. 'What! You're cradle snatching Mr Eckersley!' was Irene's reply. What amazed me afterwards when I thought about the conversation was that I was not in the slightest bit worried by Irene's comment; in fact it had all just seemed a bit of a good-humoured joke!

There were three of us at the job interview. The first person made it clear that he didn't really want the job (why on earth did he apply, I wondered?). The second person was not qualified for the post (so why did the School call her for interview I thought?). That just left me and I got the job. Nancy and I were delighted. Was it all part of God's plan?

We started making plans to get married at the end of Nancy's third year at York University. However, before our wedding, I wanted to take my Mother on one last holiday. I knew she would like to visit Scotland because she had never been there. So we set off for a week touring in my car. By then, I had sold my Mini and I now had a bright pink Ford Cortina. The holiday went well. The scenery was great, the weather fine and there was no problem with finding places to stay each night.

Then on the next to last day I looked at the road atlas, did some quick sums and saw that we could get back home easily all in one day instead of taking two days for the journey. It seemed the obvious, sensible thing to do. Yet at the back of my mind was a nagging feeling that something was not quite right. It's hard to put the feeling into words but it seemed there was a kind of dark warning that something was wrong. If you like, you could call it a premonition or a 'Silent Voice' telling me that something sinister was going to happen.

We started back on our journey to England and at first things went well and we made good progress. Then it started to rain. And suddenly, it happened. The car skidded on a wet corner, rolled over the road-side hedge and landed in the field on the other side. It all took place in a flash. Miraculously; I say that because I am sure that God was protecting us in that instant; both my Mother and I were able to climb out of the car without a scratch on either of us. We had had a remarkable escape. What made that escape even more astonishing was the fact that this took place before car seat belts had to be worn and neither of us had been strapped in.

I telephoned Nancy as soon as I could to let her know what had happened and to say that we were both safe. 'I'm so glad,' she said, 'because I have been worried about you going on the trip with your Mum in the first place.' Nancy had been concerned but had said nothing to me in case it seemed that she was trying to interfere between my Mother and myself. I understood.

The tale was not quite finished. Even more extraordinary was the fact that my Mother later told me that she, too, had had similar feelings of unease, perhaps a premonition that we were going to be in some kind of danger.

These three separate warnings were proof to me that God's Spirit is alive and active, guiding us and warning us in our everyday lives.

Nancy was living in Derwent College, one of the University Halls of Residence, and I had a flat about half a mile away. We had agreed that we would stay in York after Nancy got her degree and started investigating possible locations in the city where we might like to live.

What happened next was one of those chance(?) occurrences that would have profound long-term implications for our futures. It was a Friday night and we had been invited to a bonfire night party and fireworks celebration. But it would have meant either getting a couple of buses or scrounging a lift from someone with a car. Neither of us was keen to go but we did not want to offend the organisers. Then one of us hit on the brilliant excuse of 'going to look at a house that we are thinking of buying'. So we scoured the small ads in the 'York Evening Press', saw one going for £4,100 that seemed a possibility and there and then caught a bus and went to see it. I got a shock when we were invited in; the girl sitting in the corner was in one of my Geography classes at Queen Anne's. We liked the look of the place and agreed that we would let the owners know the following morning whether or not we would like to make an offer.

Promptly at opening time the following morning, we arrived at the Bradford Permanent Building Society office – the only one open on Saturday morning – to see if we could secure a mortgage; had a most helpful interview with the manager, who offered us a 95% mortgage instead of the usual 90%, and then rang the house owners to say 'Yes, please, we can get a loan and would like to buy the property.' We had acted in the nick of time. This was the era of rampant 'gazumping' when sellers of a property accept an offer, only to accept another higher offer days or sometimes weeks later. Our sellers had already received such another offer *that same morning* from someone in the south *who had not even seen the property*, but was prepared to pay more than we had offered. In an extraordinary act of kindness, the owners refused to accept this higher bid, saying that they had promised us first refusal.

How did we afford the £200 deposit required? It just so happened that was the amount we received from the insurers when they wrote off the Cortina that I had crashed when taking my Mother on holiday in Scotland. We both felt we had been blessed in rich measure.

Within twelve months or so, house prices for the property we had bought would double. We had been very lucky (blessed?) and 30 Howard Drive became our base for the next 28 years.

At the end of her Biology degree course at York, Nancy and I were married on 29th July 1972 at St Margaret's Church, Prestwich, in north Manchester. Guess what one of the presents was? A game of Scrabble, that regularly goes on holiday with us when we travel and was still in use nearly fifty years later.

Wedding Day – 29th July 1972

Rogues gallery

Left to right: Malcolm, Bob, Myself, John, Peter

My sister Maureen generously loaned us her Mini car for our honeymoon touring around France. Highlights included re-visiting the Eiffel Tower, a river cruise on the Seine and swimming in the Med – just about warm enough

Honeymoon: above the Dordogne valley

even for me. We had not pre-booked our bed and breakfast locations because we wanted to be fairly free with our timetable. This worked fine for most of the time, except for one night when nowhere was available. There was nothing for it; we just had to sleep in the Mini. I gave Nancy the choice of stretching out on the back seat whilst I curled around the steering wheel in the front of the car. For some reason, Nancy found great difficulty in getting to sleep; I naturally managed quite well.

With only a couple of days left, Maureen's car broke down, in Le Mans of all places. The linkage on the gears had gone and it was impossible to use either first or second gears. Le Mans is a city of steep hills, so we had a potentially serious problem. But our AA insurance cover worked brilliantly. Everything was arranged for us and we were given rail transport back to York ('repatriation' they called it) and the car arrived a few days later. What could have been a disastrous end to our honeymoon worked out greatly in our favour.

I continued teaching in York while Nancy completed an extra one-year Teaching Course, also in York. Then at the end of the school year we rented out our new house and prepared to go abroad.

EPISODE 4
Jamaica

We had decided that we both wanted to go and teach for a couple of years in one of the poorer countries of the world. This would be the second time for me and the first time for Nancy. So we started looking for possible places to think about and very soon saw a small advert in one of the newspapers asking for a Geography teacher and a Biology teacher. They were needed to work at the same school in Jamaica. Wow! Jamaica in the Caribbean! What a fabulous place to go and work. And both at the same school as well. It sounded too good to be true.

After all, we had never heard of the group, called Christians Abroad, that had put the advert in the paper and it was almost just by chance (or God's planning?) that we had seen it. We sent in our applications, heard that they wanted to see us both, and then set off to Farnham in Surrey for interview. On the train down, we spent lots of the time testing each other on questions we thought we might be asked because we both desperately wanted the interviews to go well. We need not have bothered – they virtually asked us to take up the jobs. We were delighted! We would be going to Westwood Girls High School in Stewart Town and, of course, our wedding present Scrabble would go with us.

Then followed two years of Caribbean bliss – a time of extraordinary enjoyment. Jamaica lived up to all our expectations. At least, it did after the first couple of days. 'I want to go home,' cried Nancy as she tried to accustom herself to the tropical delights of cockroaches like dinosaurs scurrying all over our room, mosquitoes giving her allergic rashes and the scorpion dropping from the ceiling onto our bed. But that soon passed and at our initial meeting with the School governors, the chairman welcomed us to 'Two years delayed honeymoon in the Caribbean'. It often seemed like that and fortunately we relished every day of our stay, knowing that the experience would never be repeated. Before we left the UK we had been recommended to read 'Four Paths to Paradise' as a suitable cultural preparation. Four Paths and Paradise, we learned, turned out to be the names of two villages in the country. 'Wait a Bit' was another delightful village place name – easily competing with some of Yorkshire's more exotic locations – and people always seemed despondent when they read in the newspaper that 'the Wait a Bit Police are investigating'.

The Geography of Jamaica fascinated us. The village of Stewart Town, we discovered much later, was originally a Maroon settlement, that is, a settlement established by runaway slaves. It lies near what was at one time the relatively inaccessible central parts of the island, reasonably close to the Cockpit Country. To a Geographer this was an amazing landscape with scores of conical hills separated by deep depressions hollowed out of the soluble limestone rock and with virtually no permanent settlement. It must have made good territory for runaways to hide in. But when we were there it was classic ganja (the local name for marijuana) country. Here the growth of marijuana was rife and every so often the Gleaner newspaper reported on how many fields of the stuff had been burnt by the police; you could tell when they had been active because the stench carried for miles. On one particular alert, The Gleaner newspaper solemnly reported that, yes, you've got it, 'The Wait a Bit police are investigating'.

The ganja traffic was, we were reliable informed, well organised. On Friday nights the electricity supply would regularly fail in Brownstown, about eight miles from where we were living. 'Ah,' said the locals, 'that means the plane has come.' The aircraft in question was presumed to have flown from Miami in Florida, landed at the Kaiser Bauxite airstrip just up the road and there collected its illicit cargo to be flown back to the United States. The business was treated with an air of resigned humour but the reality was that the ganja was traded for guns and guns fuelled the vicious gang warfare in Kingston, Jamaica's capital.

At Westwood School, Nancy had the opportunity to teach not only the full 'O' Level Biology course but also the complete 'A' Level syllabus. Her Head of Department, Joyce, was a wonderful mentor and we are still in Christmas card contact. The exams were the Cambridge Overseas papers and involved practicals in both Plant and Animal Biology. Just a few days before the exams, Cambridge would send the details of what plants and animals would be required and it was then up to the School to obtain sufficient specimens for each of the students. Nancy opened the envelope with the information and found that that particular year the girls would be expected to carry out dissections on frogs and plantains.

The frogs, for us, would be no problem, although how the Cambridge examiners expected all their other overseas centres to obtain their specimens was unclear. It was easy for us because, as well as indoor taps, we had a huge concrete 'tank' which acted as a reservoir in the garden. All the rainwater from the house roof was collected by an ingenious system of metal guttering and was then fed into the large storage tank. Uninvited, but clearly feeling it was their inalienable right, Jamaican frogs then took up residence in the tank and entertained us every evening with their beautiful melodies. But Jamaican 'frogs' were not British frogs – they were large toads, far bigger even than their British counterparts. For some reason (was it to ensure that the students did not know what their exam specimens for the following day were going to be?) the frog/toads had to be collected after nightfall. So Muggins and his wife were out in the dark with a large fishing net trying to catch the poor creatures and only having their raucous chorusing to indicate where they were swimming in the big tank. Somehow we managed to collect enough for the next day's test. But how did other schools in Jamaica, let alone in other Overseas Centres, manage to cope? Chopping up living creatures for school exams seems indefensible today, yet that's how the system operated in the early 1970s.

Collecting specimens for the plant identification/dissection proved even more problematic. Cambridge told the school that the students would be expected to cut up 'plantains'. Now 'plantains' do grow in Jamaica but they are entirely different plants from the plantains that are abundant in the UK. British plantains (Plantago) are a field weed whereas Jamaican plantains (Musa) are a big banana-like vegetable grown for its carbohydrate content and often roasted for table use. Someone at the Cambridge Examination Syndicate must have received, we assume, a metaphorical roasting for this wonderful blunder.

The Chemistry teacher at the school was Peter Spackman. He was also the curate looking after four churches in different villages as well as having a wife and four youngsters to look after. Soon after we arrived in Stewart Town and had gone to his church, Peter came up to me and said: 'You're a Christian, aren't you John? And can you read?' 'Yes, and yes' I answered. 'Good,' said Peter. 'Then I'd like you to be my Lay Reader.' So that's how

I became a Reader* in the Anglican Church. God sometimes calls us in completely unexpected ways to work for him.

Amongst the scores of memorable events, I must mention the visit of the Prime Minister to the school. Michael Manley was a charismatic figure in the countries of the Developing World. Five times married, he campaigned tirelessly on behalf of Jamaica's poor and was responsible for instituting free education in the country at primary, secondary and university levels. His visit to Westwood was therefore eagerly anticipated.

Nancy at Silver Sands beach

He was to arrive by helicopter and the plane would land on the school playing field. To create a good impression the school ancillary staff needed to go and 'bush' the field. 'Bushing' was the chopping down of the grass with machetes and in the tropical climate the grass grew rapidly. However, what had not been anticipated was that the downdraught of wind caused by the plane's rotor blades just sucked up all the cut grass and whirled it all over the place. It really was hilarious, but being visitors in a foreign country, we dared not laugh in case we caused an international incident.

The official party walked from the playing field to the school and we all took our seats waiting for the great man to speak. But what followed was utterly extraordinary. As he spoke Michael Manley **never once** looked at his audience. His gaze was fastened all the time on the windows at the side of the hall. What had happened to this charismatic dynamo? Was he afraid for his safety? Surely not, he had his bodyguards. We never discovered an explanation and it remained an unanswered mystery.

One holiday Nancy's sister Kathy came, on her own, to visit us. This was quite a courageous venture for a 16 year old and she coped extremely well with the mosquitoes, cockroaches and scorpions that had so freaked out Nancy when we had first arrived. One of the things we wanted to do was to climb Jamaica's highest mountain, Blue Mountain Peak (7,402 feet) in the Blue Mountains where Jamaica's famous coffee is grown. Kathy was keen to come with us. It would be by far the highest mountain that both she and Nancy had ever climbed. There is a well-established walking track and it is about six miles to the summit. From the top, if the weather is clear, it's possible to see both north and south sides of the island. Unfortunately, it was cloudy when we were there but that did not take away our sense of achievement.

Blue Mountain Peak (7,402 feet) taken by Kathy

On another occasion Nancy and I had been walking in the Blue Mountain country and had experienced a tropical storm. This is not as bad as a hurricane but was still quite alarming. We had walked only a short distance from the hut where we were staying before having to turn back and in that brief time, half a dozen fast flowing streams had suddenly appeared. It was a vivid reminder of the dangers that many people in Jamaica have to face when a real hurricane strikes.

Inevitably we missed some important family events whilst we were in Jamaica. Nancy's parents had their 25th Wedding Anniversary and her brother Peter married Pam. My sister Maureen was married to Bill and they promptly went off to settle on the other side of the world in New Zealand – not bad for a lass who'd said she never wanted to leave Liverpool. And Nancy's grandmother died. Her Dad telegraphed the sad news to us but we never received the message. Later on an airmail letter asked why we had not responded. 'We know nothing about it,' we replied. So we made regular checks at the village post office but they continued to tell us that nothing had arrived. Nancy's Dad got increasingly frustrated about how poor the telegraph services were .... until he at last realised that he had sent the message to 'Nancy Carter', forgetting his dear daughter had changed her name when we had got married. Ah well, such things happen at times of stress.

Naturally we tried to make as much as we could of the opportunities for travelling whilst we were in the West Indies. As well as some delightful trips to different parts of Jamaica itself, we managed a Greyhound bus journey up the east coast of the USA and an eye-opening holiday in Mexico.

However, the most memorable trip, for both good and bad memories, was the island-hopping cruise we completed around the Leeward and Windward Islands aboard the **Federal Maple** banana boat. The general plan was to sail between islands during the night and then have the daytime to explore each new island. You could hardly call it a 'cruise' because we opted to travel as 'Deck' rather than as 'Cabin' passengers because that was so much cheaper. There were separate male and female dormitories (Nancy remembers the women slept in three level bunks.)

We set sail on Maundy Thursday and almost from the word go, we were both terribly sea-sick. On the first night the crew had a party – presumably got drunk – and then forgot to switch on the bilge pumps. The following morning the dormitories were under water; Nancy remembers it being nearly a foot deep in the women's block. The crew was hauled out on parade and received a right telling off. Nancy saw this but I was lying on my bed moaning and being sick.

Good Friday and Holy Saturday we spent hardly able to speak to each other, unable to eat (although Nancy did manage to take some dry ship's biscuits) and being tormented as the ship's cooks walked past us with hot, steaming dishes of stew that Cabin passengers were well enough to eat. Then on Easter Sunday we made terra firma at our first island – St Kitts – and everything changed. It was a real Easter Resurrection type transformation. Thereafter we had a marvellous week.

St Kitts is only tiny and we took a trip round the island before stopping for afternoon tea at a small café in the capital. 'Mind if I join you?' said a friendly looking local who came across and introduced himself as the Prime Minister of the island. Gulping on our biscuits, we managed to maintain our decorum, listened politely (but disbelievingly) to his story and then he got up to leave. 'Oh, by the way,' he added showing us a souvenir magazine he had with him, 'here's a picture of myself with Her Majesty Queen Elizabeth.' His tale had been true after all.

Antigua, with its 365 beaches, boasting a different one for every day of the year, was next on the itinerary, followed by Montserrat, nick-named the Emerald Isle of the Caribbean partly because of the Irish ancestry of many of the inhabitants. The south of the island is now virtually uninhabited after the devastating volcanic eruption of the 1990s.

Dominica came next, with its tropical rain forest and natural hot springs. It once had thriving lime tree plantations providing the fruit for Roses lime juice. Then we reached St Lucia which claims to be the only island in the world to have a 'Drive in Volcano' and we just had to be proper tourists and hire a taxi to experience this particular treat. What the tourist blurbs did not prepare you for was the stench of sulphur coming out of the crater. 'It stinks like rotten eggs' is a fair description.

Unlike the other islands, Barbados is not volcanic but formed of coral limestone and in some people's eyes, with its afternoon tea and cricket, is 'just like England'. St Vincent soon followed and then in Grenada we saw women involved in the terribly laborious task of shelling nutmegs, 'Grenada's Gold'. Three parts of the fruit are used: the outer pericarp to make jelly, the red membrane inside called mace and the nutmeg seed itself used in making oils, butter and medicine.

When we finally reached Trinidad, the Federal Maple was behind schedule and we had no time for exploring it, the largest of the islands on our route. We had to catch the first plane back to Jamaica since we were already late for the start of term.

Our 'two years extended honeymoon', as the Chair of the School Governors had described our time in Jamaica, ended in 1975. Nancy wrote an incredibly long letter to her Mum and Dad detailing just about everything we had done, said, heard, seen, eaten or planned during the previous week. She left just a tiny space at the foot of the letter to squeeze in very small print 'Oh, and by the way, just in case you're interested, God willing, you should be grandparents in November!'

Of course they were absolutely delighted at the news and nearly as excited as we were.

Lay Reader' is an old term meaning someone who is allowed to preach, lead services and carry out various other activities in the Church but is not ordained as a priest.

EPISODE 5
Family – we become six – then nineteen

We came back from Jamaica to our house in York that we had rented out before we left for the Caribbean and we now set about the serious business of acquiring babies. Roger, Peter, Tanya and Sharon appeared in quick succession. This was in the days before Dads did much of the baby-minding work and I was out of the house in the daytime anyway. So it was Nancy who was left to do all the nappy changing, the feeding, the trips to playschool, doctors and school concerts; not to mention keeping the builders happy with tea and coffee as they converted our two-bedroom bungalow into something just about twice the size.

I had managed to keep reasonably fit running in Jamaica and was able to take up racing again with Rowntrees Athletic Club. The Three Peaks Race was still a big attraction and Nancy recalls one race (I think it was probably my last) when I flopped exhausted over the finishing line, only for a well-meaning official trying immediately to get me on my feet again. Nancy maintains that I, very impolitely, told the official to leave me alone. Needless to say, I have no such recollection.

I mentioned Dennis Weir in Episode 3. With his encouragement I had started road-running and while living in York I managed my first marathon, called the 'Maxol', in Manchester. I did what I thought was a reasonable time for me – I think it was 2 hours 43 minutes for the 26 miles. But it was my second marathon that I remember most. This race was in May 1976 (so I was 33 years old then). It happened to be the selection race for the 1976 Olympics, so I thought 'Hey, this will sound good when I tell the children that I ran in an Olympic qualifying race!' But, to be truthful, anybody could enter the race; you didn't have to be particularly good. Anyway, to cut a 26 mile story short, I had a terrible race. You may have heard the expression that runners sometimes use about 'hitting the wall'. This means that they reach a stage in a race when suddenly they feel as if they have hit a brick wall. They can't go on any further and they have to stop. In marathon races, this 'wall' often comes at about the 20 mile mark, when the runners still have another five or six miles to go. Well, I started feeling tired after only about five miles, so it wasn't looking too good for the rest of the race. I got gradually worse so that when I hit the wall at about 20 miles, I wanted to give up, drop out and go home. But I couldn't because Nancy wouldn't let me! She had been following the race around the roads in our car, so that she could give me encouragement every few miles. 'No! You're not giving up yet!' she kept saying mile after mile, 'keep going; you can do it!' Secretly, I was very glad of the encouragement Nancy was giving me because without her I would never have finished my Olympic selection marathon. So I did keep going and, this is the really important bit, I was so enormously thankful to Nancy that I promised to buy her a new dress. That just shows how grateful I was for her encouragement.

Eventually I finished the race in a disappointing time of 3 hours, 13 minutes and 43 seconds. But at least I'd be able to tell the grandchildren that I had come 213th In the Olympic selection race.

Oh, I nearly forgot: do you know, Nancy has **still** not chosen that new dress I promised her even after all these years.

Here are a few more stories from the family archives.

The Greenhouse that Flew Away

Nancy is very talented when it comes to doing creative things. As well as preaching, she can draw and paint, she can sing and play different musical instruments, she can dance and play act, she can dress-make and she has done pottery work. The only one of those things that I can faintly attempt to do is play acting so Nancy thought I should try to learn some new skills and she encouraged me to try making things for the garden.

I must admit, I have greatly enjoyed doing garden woodwork and have gained much pleasure from some of the things I have made over the years, usually in the summer holidays. Don't get the wrong idea, though. They are nothing fancy or complicated; more like 'bash it and bodge it' creations. But it's been good fun.

My first garden project was the greenhouse. We went to one of the DIY stores to get ideas about how their greenhouses had been built, then came home and drew our own plans. It had to be a plastic greenhouse because we thought glass would make it too heavy. I bought the wood for all the framework, cut it to the right size, painted it and screwed it all together. Then I fixed all the see-through plastic windows to the frame, made sure the door swung open easily on its hinges and remembered to let the windows open properly. When it was all finished, I was really pleased – we could now actually start growing some plants in it.

Unfortunately, a few days later there was a heavy storm with strong winds and, while we were asleep, the whole greenhouse was lifted up by the wind, blown over the hedge and then dumped on to next door's lawn! Oh dear. I had learnt an important basic lesson: always make sure your greenhouse is **firmly** and very **securely** anchored to the ground.

I must tell you about a special Eckersley game that the boys invented and played when they were young. As far as I know no-one else in the whole world plays it, which is a great pity because it is so simple to organise and yet brings enormous enjoyment when it is played. The game is called **GUKOS**. That stands for **German United Kick-Off Slipper**. Here's how it goes.

Roger and Peter were about six or seven years old and it was the time of the football World Cup. The lads were full of enthusiastic interest and knew that Germany had been England's traditional rivals since England beat Germany way back in the 1966 World Cup Final.

Nancy was out for the evening and I was responsible for looking after the children. I'd put the girls to bed and the boys had a little extra time before they, too, had to go to bed. They said they wanted to play GUKOS. 'How do you play?' I asked them. 'It's easy, Dad, we'll show you', they said.

There are two teams, but only one player on each side. The two players sit on the floor on opposite sides of the room – a living room is probably best because that's usually a bit bigger than the dining room or kitchen. And there's more likely to be a photo or a painting or some other picture hanging on the sitting room walls than in the kitchen.

Roger sat on one side of the room, Peter on the other, and above each was their picture. (To be honest, I can't remember what the pictures were showing but that doesn't matter because any old picture will do.) The pictures represent the goals, so they have to be roughly the same size as each other to make things fair. 'It's like a penalty shoot-out, Dad' the lads explained. 'The idea is to 'shoot' your kick-off slipper across the room and hit the target on the other side. That counts as scoring a goal.'

'What amazingly inventive sons I have!' I said to myself in proud admiration. 'I could never have thought of such a wonderfully creative idea!'

The lads seemed really clever with their GUKOS skills – I guessed they'd probably been training very seriously without my knowing. And the excitement! It was nail-biting stuff: first England took the lead, then Germany 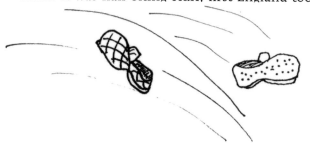 equalised, then England scored again! The atmosphere was electric!

Suddenly .... in walked Nancy. She was horrified! She went ballistic! **'What on earth is going on?'** she demanded. 'Up to

'Picture, picture on the wall – who is the most mischievous of all?'
(Clockwise: Roger, Peter, Sharon, Tanya)

bed immediately!' she ordered the boys. But she never told them off; no; instead she blamed **me**, the innocent spectator and said I should have known better!

That was the end of GUKOS, never to be played again. The rules were only explained to the girls years later in case they thought about taking up the challenge. Oh, and Nancy gave me **two** black marks on the Trouble-making Chart.

Nancy had instituted the idea of **Family Star Charts**. These were Star Charts for Good Behaviour with gold and silver stars being awarded for being helpful; but there were also Trouble-making black marks given for mischievous trouble-making. Now at this point I should explain that I don't agree with the rest of the family. I am absolutely **certain** that I deserved most of the gold and silver stars. Yet Nancy, Roger, Peter, Tanya and Sharon are convinced that I was undoubtedly the champion of the Trouble-making Black Marks. Fancy, both sides can't be right. I wonder whose side of the story you think is nearest to the truth?

Let me tell you about one example of Nancy's Trouble-making. It was Christmas time and our good friends from Church, Sean and Linda, had come round on Christmas afternoon for tea. Nancy had asked Linda to buy three new shirts for Nancy to give to me as presents. So, not suspecting a thing, I opened the parcels and took the three shirts out of their boxes with everyone looking on excitedly. I looked at the shirts and I couldn't believe my eyes – they were awful! Absolutely terrible! One was covered all over with red spots, one with yellow spots and the third had pink, yes, **pink** spots all over it! What could I say? These were presents chosen by someone I thought was one of our best friends. If I told the truth and said 'Linda, they're awful' she might never speak to me again. On the other hand if I said 'Linda, thank you very much for choosing such lovely, thoughtful presents for Nancy to give to me, I do like them' then I'd be telling a whopping big lie. Nancy, Sean and Linda could hardly stop themselves from bursting out laughing as they watched me squirming. Eventually, they had pity on me and explained. It was all a big joke. The shirts were real enough but the spots that were covered all over them were small pieces of round sticky coloured paper that Nancy had cut out and then stuck on the shirts. It must have taken ages to prepare but it was well worth the time and effort. It was all great fun and I, of course, laughed with everyone else. But it meant that Nancy was, without any question, Queen of Trouble-making Black Marks.

Being able to laugh at yourself is a great gift to have and I'm pleased to say that both of us are able to do that. Teasing each other in a kind, gentle way can be good fun. But it must never be unkind or hurtful.

Interlude

Perhaps it's time for me to tell you something more about my **Mother and Dad**.

All my memories of Mother are wonderfully positive. She struggled hard to bring up Maureen and myself in our early years under very difficult circumstances and then when we were at school she was always supporting us at by coming to sports days, school plays and concerts, testing us on our homework and on our lines for school plays.

Then in 1985 Mother had a heart attack – followed soon after by another. This second one proved fatal and Mother died. But she was not afraid of dying. At Sunday School as a child she had sung the words of the chorus

'Jesus loves me, this I know, For the Bible tells me so'

And that belief sustained her throughout her life. So, after the heart attacks, she was not afraid of dying; her strong faith made her sure that death was only the gateway to another totally different existence with God. In fact, she once told me that she thought of death as being the start of what she called 'a Great New Adventure'.

When Mother died, I had expected that I would have been able to take the shock reasonably calmly. Yes, of course, I knew that I would be terribly sad, but at least I would have the consolation that Mother would be alive with God in a better world and that one day in the future we would meet again.

But death and the loss of loved ones don't follow simple logical expectations. I reacted in a completely different way from the way I had anticipated. Dad sent me to buy the flowers for the funeral and everything seemed to be going to plan when, totally out of the blue, it suddenly hit me. I had to sit down on the nearby Church steps and I cried bucketsful. The same thing happened a few days later at the funeral service itself. I just had to sit down and cry – making a lot of noise but people, I'm glad to say, were very understanding.

Bereavement can hit us in all sorts of ways for which we are not prepared. But there is nothing wrong about weeping; it's a sign of our love for someone. And Jesus wept at the grave of his friend Lazarus.

• • •

Another chapter in life was about to begin. Now that Mother had died, how would my Dad cope on his own? He had said on numerous occasions that he wanted to stay living in Liverpool and had no wish to come to York to be nearer to Nancy and me. He had all his friends at the Nag's Head pub where he went nearly every night and apart from us, he knew no-one in York and so he thought he would be terribly lonely.

However, a mile away from us there was some sheltered housing accommodation at a place called Guardian Court and a flat had become vacant. We persuaded Dad to come across and 'Just look at it – there's absolutely no pressure to say you'd like to live there'.

So Dad came, he looked and – there and then – he declared 'Yes, I'll have it!' Nancy and I were flabbergasted – we couldn't believe our ears. Dad had been so determined to stay in Liverpool that his change of heart seemed like a miracle to us.

It seemed no time at all before Dad was in his new home, just a few minutes away from us so we could visit regularly. But soon we noticed a problem; he kept going back to Liverpool. Had we made some terrible mistake, we wondered. Fortunately, we soon found out the reason.

Mother and Dad had been good friends with another couple, Ellis and Olwyn ('Ollie') who lived nearby them in Liverpool. A short time before, Ellis had died, leaving Ollie a widow. You can probably guess what comes next .... Dad and Ollie started seeing more of each other and within a year decided that they wanted to get married. It might have sounded like a very quick romance but, after all, they had known each for a good number of years. And how could I have possibly objected when I had proposed to Nancy after we'd been going out together for only three months, most of which time, she reminds me, she was in York and I was in Manchester?! Scary, isn't it, when you think of some of the risky things you do when you're young (and in love as Tanya adds).

And so it was. We were delighted at the prospect of a wedding in the family and were pleased that Mo and Bill, away on the other side of the world in New Zealand, were happy with the idea as well. Preparations for the Big Day went ahead and to my great delight, Dad asked me to be his Best Man. 'Best Man at your father's wedding'? That sounded really good; how could I possibly refuse?

It was a very happy occasion; the bride bloomed; the four grandchildren behaved impeccably; Nancy composed (and sang) a special song and I was able to offer my Dad some helpful hints about the recipe for a happy married life. You know the sort of thing – always choose your words very carefully: 'Yes, Dear', 'No Dear', 'Certainly Dear', 'Anything you say Dear'. The recipe, you'll no doubt realise, that I always use with Nancy.

Dad and Ollie had four years of happy life together before Dad died peacefully in hospital in 1990. Maureen had phoned from New Zealand and spoken with him just a few hours before he passed away. Ollie remained in Guardian Court until she died in 1999. She had been great company and had fitted into our family extraordinarily well. The second marriage had, we thought, been extremely beneficial for both of them.

At Ernie and Ollie's Wedding

Back to the Family

Family life continued to bring fresh excitements almost every day. With four youngsters and all their interests and requirements it also became more complicated. So what follows must necessarily be only a brief summary of some of the most memorable highlights.

Roger (then 8) and Peter (then 7) came camping with me for three days in the summer of **1983** and they loved it. They seemed to rise to a challenge: 'Ruth and Helen walked ten miles last holiday – I bet you couldn't do that.' *Without a word*, off we went and completed the walk without so much as a murmur. 'Ruth and Helen' were a few years older than Roger and Peter; but they were girls!

The boys were becoming, much to their father's consternation, real Yorkshire lads. When John and Liz Crompton, over from America in **1984**, called with their two girls, they couldn't stop themselves doubling up with the giggles at the thought of eating 'plaern caerk wi' pep'min' fillin'.

Roger, I think it was in **1988,** cracked a bone in his leg whilst on a school trip. He had been jumping down from a basketball net in the gym. Back home he tested his Dad's patience:

'Roger; you're **not** to skateboard down the new concrete drive while your leg's still in plaster – and I don't care whether you're using your crutches or not!'

In **1989**, after two years' training, Nancy was ordained Deacon on 2nd July in York Minster – a most important step in her life.

After several years of complaining about sitting on cold Northumbrian beaches wearing coats and hats, the children finally persuaded us to have a holiday in Cornwall. Squeezing four youngsters into the back of our car was a bit of a tight fit but we managed, albeit with some inevitable complaints and trouble making. One of the highlights for the five youngest members of the family was the surfing. The most senior member maintained an informed, knowledgeable eye over the efforts of the other five and then proceeded to offer helpful, advisory comments, gently reminding them of how he had surfed 20 years previously onto a deserted white coral beach in the hot tropical waters of the Indian Ocean. The rest of the family seemed, albeit a little reluctantly, somewhat impressed but nevertheless demanded a demonstration. Despite all the experienced one's protestations, he had to bow to popular pressure and make an attempt to prove his, admittedly long unpractised, skills. Alas, it wasn't at all the same, 20 years on, in a cold, crowded, polluted little bit of the Atlantic Ocean. But he was still the only one of the family who could claim to have ever climbed Kilimanjaro.

I explained the Family 'Trouble-making Chart' earlier. A note in the family records says that in **1990** J (aka 'TMJ – Trouble-making Jern') scored exceptionally highly, not by doing anything overtly troublesome, but just by dropping hints, peering at the newspaper ads and muttering indistinctly into his beard about the possibility of changing cars and trading in 'Bluebell', the old blue Ital Estate, for a replacement second-hand ... Lada! Well, what an outcry this caused. The lads threatened to leave home; the girls cried that they would have absolutely no street cred whatsoever. And Nancy sided with her four offspring rather than her husband.

In fact, the new car was not bought until four years later and by now the choice had become a red Skoda ('Rosebud') and that was nearly as bad in the kids' eyes as a Lada. Yet Skoda had been taken over by Volkswagen and so I could boast that I had a 'Volkswagen-subsidiary' vehicle. They were not impressed. But it made an excellent topic for School Assembly – 'Why should you be duped into believing all the advertisers' lies and half-truths?' Yet I admit that I had to smile at the Skoda joke going around at the time: 'What's the difference between a Skoda and a golf ball?' Answer: 'You can drive a golf ball more than a hundred yards.'

The Sink that Broke Itself

In our house in Howard Drive we had a delightful mint green bathroom suite – bath, toilet and hand wash basin. It looked lovely but one day we found that the washer on the hand basin tap needed changing. 'That should be no problem,' I said confidently to Nancy, 'leave it in my safe hands. So I got the tools and things ready and started the job. But ... calamity ... somehow the heavy spanner leapt out of my hand and flung itself into the basin with a loud crash. Oh dear, the spanner had made a little crack in the basin. Nancy said it would have to be changed.

We made enquiries about getting a new lovely mint green wash basin. But they no longer made bathroom suites in that colour. What could we do?

We would either have to have a white one (Nancy said that was no good because it wouldn't match the green toilet and green bath) or we would have to buy a complete new suite of hand basin, toilet and bath.

'But that means we'll have to throw away a perfectly good toilet and a perfectly good bath!' Horror of horrors! I couldn't even think of being so wasteful. What was the answer?

'I know,' I said, 'We have three choices.

(1) we can try Sellotape (Nancy ignored that suggestion)

(2) we can wait till it mends itself (she wasn't keen on that either)

(3) or we can pray about it (she thought I might have been serious).'

We decided to compromise: we'd try (2) and (3). So we went off to bed and slept on it.

It was early May when all this happened. I know that because it was Christian Aid Week and I was going round the local houses delivering and collecting Christian Aid Week envelopes. A day or so after the heavy spanner had misbehaved itself, I had to go to a certain nearby road (I daren't tell you its name) to collect that road's envelopes.

You'll never guess; I'm certain you'll never guess; what was in the skip outside one of the houses. It was a mint green hand wash basin – exactly the same size, shape and shade of green that ours was! It looked in perfect condition. I couldn't believe my eyes.

I rushed home to tell Nancy. 'Where is it then? Why didn't you bring it home with you?' she demanded in amazement. 'It was too big and heavy to carry on my own,' I said. 'Well you better go straight back in the car and collect it,' my beloved replied. 'But make sure you ask first to see if you can take it.'

So off I went in the car to see if I could save a beautiful piece of bathroom furniture from being sent to a miserable end in the Council tip. I got to the house, knocked on the door, not too loudly in case the people inside actually heard me, and waited for an answer. But no-one came to the door. 'Oh dear,' I thought, 'whatever shall I do?'

It didn't take me too long to make up my mind. 'In the interests of recycling a piece of beautiful bathroom furniture,' I told myself, 'I think it my civic duty to rescue it from a horrible death at the Council tip.' So, very carefully, I lifted the basin from the top of the skip, placed it gently in the boot of the car and then drove back home. I felt ever so virtuous at having being able to save and recycle a perfectly adorable piece of exquisite bathroom furniture.

We paid a plumber to take out the old basin and to put our 'new' one in place in the bathroom. 'We'll never have another wash basin like it,' I said proudly to Nancy. 'Right Love,' she replied. So that's all finished, we agreed.

But actually it wasn't. A few weeks later, our Vicar, Robin, had asked Nancy if she would go to a nearby family and do a Baptism Preparation visit to explain what Baptism means. She agreed, got the address from Robin and went to meet the family. The meeting went very well and the family were friendly. They were interested in what Nancy had to say about Baptism and then they started chatting generally about how they enjoyed living in such a nice place as Rawcliffe.

'But do you know,' said one of them suddenly, 'a few weeks ago we had the most unusual experience. We had been replacing our bathroom suite and had put the old one into a skip outside the house ready for collection and for taking away to be broken up at the Council tip. Lo and behold, when we got up in the morning the entire washbasin had disappeared!'

"It's Astonishing How Personal Possessions Accumulate!"

'Really!' exclaimed Nancy, wide-eyed with astonishment and nearly choking on her biscuit. 'Isn't it amazing what spooky things can happen even in a nice, quiet place like Rawcliffe?'

You will have guessed by now that I am a great believer in recycling. Part of me thinks that it's just silly throwing things away when they still have a useful life and part of me believes that it's wrong to keep using up the Earth's resources when we don't have to. In fact, I'm a great believer in keeping things 'in case they come in useful' and this motto has become a favourite saying in our family.

It's a long time ago now but one year our friends Sean and Linda (the ones you met in the Spotty Shirts story) gave me a present of a wonderful cartoon picture (see above) by Norman Thelwell which they thought summed up my character.

I found it hilarious. On one level it illustrated so well Jesus' warning 'not to store up treasure on earth, where rust destroys and thieves break in and steal'. Can you just imagine robbers coming in the middle of the night, piling all the Travellers' scrap metal onto their truck and then flogging it to some shady metal dealer – they'd make a small fortune. Yet on the other hand, Sean recognised my sincere concern not to destroy things 'that might come in useful' – and do I imagine it, or has that bath in the right centre of the picture, a beautiful mint green colour?

51

1992 I reached the half-century milestone. One kind friend wrote on the card signed by those at church: 'Fifty indeed! You certainly don't look it!' Another wag added, 'but I'm sure you must have done at one time!' Grrrr

1993 My summer projects so far had included the greenhouse, a garden table and benches, a concrete driveway, a bikeport and other civil engineering follies. Then 1993 saw the construction of Penelope, the most demanding so far. Nancy had been offered the paid part-time post of Lay Training Officer in the Church. She needed an office of her own, rather than sharing the small study with the piano players and her incredibly well-organised, meticulously tidy husband with his various piling systems scattered around the floor. We thought about the possibility of a further extension to the back of the house but this was an unrealistic non-starter. Then in a flash of inspiration, we hit on the idea of banishing Nancy to a hut at the bottom of the garden. Please note: not just any old hut, rather a super de-luxe version appropriate to a Lady of the Cloth. So the shed, christened 'Penelope' by Nancy as befits a future Woman Priest's ecclesiastical office suite, was born into the world. The archive letter notes that it was, surprisingly, peppered with less frustration than either of us had expected and we had three weeks of great enjoyment constructing it. We chose a reasonably priced chalet-type garden shed, we lagged ceiling and walls with fibreglass insulation, covered the inside walls with white melamine-faced hardboard, carpeted the floor, put up shelves, had a friend install electricity and finally installed the word processor. A thermostat controlled electric greenhouse fan heater ensured it did not get too damp in winter. It worked like a treat.

1994 In the spring Tanya and Sharon agreed to walk the Dales Way with Nancy and myself; the boys staying at home. This proved to be highly successful with both girls coping extremely well and we averaged 10 miles a day. We used the two-car method so that we were able to return to base, a hired caravan in Grassington, each day. This is extravagant in terms of petrol consumption but it does mean that you don't need to back-pack with a week's gear in your rucksacks every day and we didn't want to put the girls off walking. When they returned to school, Sharon had difficulty in persuading her class-mates (and teacher) that she had completed the walk but she coped extremely well and it must have given her confidence to walk the Wolds Way with me, in stages over several weeks, some years later. Apart from some poor weather on a couple of days, there was really only one thing that spoiled it – it's the story of 'The Dog'.

We had parked one of the cars at a farm overnight with the idea of collecting it the following morning. It just so happened that one of the farmer's sheepdogs had just given birth to pups and the farmer needed to sell some of them. Tanya fell madly in love with them. *'Please,'* she begged, 'can we have one – just one?' But there was no way Nancy or I would countenance the prospect. Despite all our efforts to argue logically the practicalities of adding dog ownership to the work of bringing up four youngsters, Tanya was near inconsolable. Poor Tan. I had forgotten the next bit but Tanya reminds me that, as a consequence of her parents' intransigence, her sulks and disappointment transferred into an aggressive power walking pace for the rest of the week.

However, as I am writing this now, she has at last achieved her dream. Some 30-odd years on, she, Phil and her family have just bought their own dog and, so far, they are enjoying the delights of three-times-a-day dog walking.

On a lighter note, having walked the Dales Way proved a valuable preparation for my using the route for the school sponsored relay race the following year.

1995 This was a hinge point time in our family life. Roger and Peter escaped the embarrassment of the new Skoda by leaving the nest for University, Roger (who had taken a year out) going to Lancaster and Peter to Newcastle. Both seem to cope with the harsh rigours of academia: boozin', partyin', clubbin' and so on. Tanya settled into 6th Form and playing hockey; Sharon started GCSEs; was thinking of the possibility of Nursery Nursing work and was doing a sterling job as helper with children's work at Clifton Moor Church.

1997 Tanya started at Leicester University studying Social and Economic History, while Sharon began her Nursery Nursing Course at York College.

Celebrating our 25th Wedding Anniversary at St Mark's Church in 1997

25th Wedding Anniversary Paris

This year also saw Nancy and me celebrating our **25th Wedding Anniversary** and we decided to have a special Renewal of Wedding Vows service taken by our Vicar, Robin Fletcher. All the family attended and afterwards the four offspring treated everyone to a superb dine-out dinner all arranged by themselves. It was an excellent day in all ways. Later Nancy and I splashed out with a second honeymoon in Paris – in a hotel, of all places!

1998 There was much rejoicing at the safe arrival of our first grandchild – Andrew John being born to Tanya and Phil. Guess when? On Nancy's birthday. She could not have asked for a better present. The following year they became first-time house owners.

2000 After the sad death of Ollie the year before, the Millennium was an exceptionally memorable year for our family. It was amazingly busy in all sorts of ways; certainly a year we would not forget in a hurry. In addition to Nancy taking up her appointment as Vicar of Heslington, Sharon passed her driving test as well as her Nursery Nursing Diploma and got a job in York just before we moved.

Tanya and Phil were married in the summer and became Mr and Mrs Willis. It really was a great day; everything went exactly as it ought – the groom was totally composed, the bride was late, the bride's mother cried and 18 month old Andy nearly stole the show.

Roger landed a very attractive job right in the middle of London, while Peter managed to obtain

Tanya and Phil

funding for a Master's degree back in Newcastle. And the new Vicar of Heslington became a quinquagenarian (what a nice word to drop casually into the conversation).

2001 Beth Willis born

2003 was a year of house moving for three of the offspring: Roger and Karen purchased a flat in Balham; Peter and Susannah moved to, and bought in Newcastle; Sharon joined with Nancy and myself to buy 48 Burlington Avenue ('Burlo'). There was asbestos to rip out, the whole house to re-wire, new ceilings to put in, plus plastering, tiling and decorating to complete the renovation. But Sharon had a place to call her own.

2004 Nancy's Dad, Brian, died peacefully in his sleep from an aneurism. His sudden death was totally unexpected and a great shock but he was spared any suffering. I was amazed at Nancy's composure in being able to speak at his funeral.

James Willis born

Roger and Karen started what was planned as their 'Round the World Bike Ride'. This included Scandinavia and a good deal of Eastern Europe. However, they reluctantly decided that the risks of cycling through the Middle East were too great and so had to abandon that idea.

They did, however, cycle almost the full length of New Zealand and camper-vanned in Australia. Perhaps they were now thinking of settling down?

Andrew, James and Beth

2006 Roger and Karen got married in July; followed quickly by Peter and Susannah in August

Roger and Karen

2007 To our great delight, Tanya became confirmed in Leicester.

Roger and Karen went – literally – cheetah walking and slept with cheetahs – on a fabulous eye-opening trip to Namibia.

Susannah successfully completed her PhD and so this year there were five differently titled ladies in the clan – Rev Nancy, Ms/Miss Sharon, Mrs Karen, Doctor Susannah, Tanya Willis (née Eckersley). The males remained staunchly Mr Men.

Peter and Susannah

2008 Sharon finished walking the Wolds Way with me and then more grandchildren arrived in quick succession:

2008 Abigail born to Peter and Susannah

2009 Lucy born to Roger and Karen

2010 Leia born to Sharon and Stuart

2011 After Nancy and I had completed our LEJOG Walk (see Episode 10), we took up residence in Flamborough. Our new home was a small, one-bedroomed bungalow at the end of a quiet cul-de-sac. However, we saw that it had the potential for a loft extension, very similar to that which we had made in Rawcliffe, so we went ahead and bought it. When we finished LEJOG, we got a small firm to carry out the extension into the roof. They were an excellent outfit. However, at the end of the building operations, there was a huge pile of heavy duty, smooth-planed offcut wood left after the new beams had been cut to their required lengths. All this 'waste', we were told had to be either burned or dumped. Naturally, I was horrified. I could see the builder's point of view; for every loft extension they constructed there was always a great amount of unwanted surplus offcuts for which they had no place to store. Our extension was only a small affair and I shuddered to think of the total waste being generated by scores of building companies working on larger projects. The inevitable happened; I reclaimed the 'waste', used some immediately for new projects and stored the rest in the garage 'until it came in useful'. Come in useful it certainly did, my prize creation being 'The Grandad Bench' for which I cajoled Andrew, Beth and James to lend willing(?) help. Some of the surplus was even transported to Leicester for use on Tan and Phil's allotment.

2012 Charlie born to Roger and Karen
and Lukas born to Peter and Susannah

This was also the year Nancy and I celebrated our 40th (Ruby) Wedding Anniversary. All the family joined in the celebration which, on a lovely sunny day, included all sorts of 'garden sports'. By popular demand, yours truly subjected himself to the indignities of 'All Pile on Grandad' which was a kind of latter-day 'All Pile on Daddy' which our four had played 20 years or so before. Egged on by – I'm *sure* it must have been Roger – and aided and

Charlie and Lucy

Abigail and Lukas

abetted by their Nan, the grandkids seemed to have no trouble in immediately acquiring the skills of the game. Unfortunately, the Trouble-making Star Chart was nowhere to be found.

2014 was a difficult one for Nancy's Mum. After her mild stroke the previous Christmas, she had gall stones removed (nowadays taken out by key-hole surgery), pleurisy, the removal of two skin cancers and a cataract operation. Nevertheless she remained feistily* positive at all times and still played a mean hand at cards.

A big family event was my sister Maureen and husband Bill's Ruby Wedding Anniversary. As part of their celebrations, they came over from New Zealand and stayed for a week with us as well as touring round the country. They wanted Nancy and myself to share a celebratory Ruby Wedding meal with them but somehow our offspring got wind of the idea and decided it would be a wonderful idea if they and the grandchildren could share in the merriment and meal as well. Can't imagine where they get such brass neck from ...

There were two very sad incidents in **2015**. The first was the death in July of our brother-in-law John, married to Nancy's sister Kathy. John was the archetypal 'bigger-than-life' figure and a man of many gifts who, in the words of St John's Gospel, had lived 'life in all its fullness'. We, and Kathy of course, miss him greatly.

In the following month, Sharon lost the baby she was expecting. Isabel was actually born alive at 21 weeks but died within a few minutes. Help for parents in such situations has improved enormously since Nancy was a chaplain at York Hospital and Sharon and Stuart received excellent pastoral support.

By **2016** Nancy and I reckoned that we had both reached that stage of life when 'Time' seems to have acquired a new dimension – we call it 'Time Warpism'. You probably know the sort of thing we've got in mind: 'You mean it was only this year that Sharon and Stuart got married?!' And yes it was, in February – on Sharon's birthday. Great excitement had been in evidence over the choosing and purchase of wedding garments – for some reason I was left out of the deliberations.

---

* not in the Scrabble dictionary, in case you're wondering

The other great event was the **safe birth of Natasha** in late summer.

Sharon and Stuart

After Sharon's experience the previous year of losing Isabel, there was more than the usual apprehension about Natasha's arrival. So everyone was relieved at the happy outcome and once again reminded of the extraordinary good fortune we have of being blessed with the magnificent services of our NHS. Sibling Leia (then six years old and an experienced Year 2 Primary Schooler) was delighted in having 'my little sister' but couldn't for the life of

Leia and Natasha

her understand why Natasha didn't want to wake up and spend all day playing with her big sister instead of just sleeping all the time. But we were sure she would learn.

In **2018** Tanya resigned from teaching, fed up, I think it's fair to say, with Government overload and bureaucracy. However, she quickly found great satisfaction and fulfilment setting up her own gardening business as well as appreciating the release from teaching pressures.

It was this year that Maureen and Bill came to visit us again from New Zealand. Maureen had arranged a mind-boggling itinerary through Scotland and England and then came to us for a rest. As always it was great to meet up again, this time for a week in July.

Nancy's Mum Barbara celebrated her 90th Birthday in September. She was pleased that all the family (34 of us in total) were able to come for the festivities. Nancy's sister, Kathy, lives just round the corner from her and is her official carer and keeps a daily eye on her. We see them both about once a week.

EPISODE 6
Harrogate

At first when we came back to York from Jamaica I had not been able to get a local teaching job in York so I spent six months working at Terry's chocolate factory. It was a very happy atmosphere and I enjoyed the change of environment. Then in the following spring of 1976, I obtained interviews on successive days for two Geography teaching posts. The first was 20 miles or so away at St Aidan's Church of England Comprehensive in Harrogate. The second, on the following day, was for a head of department position at a girls' school in York, obviously a much more accessible location. I was offered the Harrogate job but then asked the interview panel if I could postpone my decision because of my other interview on the following day. They said no. What a dilemma! I demurred for a few minutes and then made up my mind. 'Yes, please, I said. 'I'll take the bird in the hand and accept your kind offer!' I'd never heard of C of E Comprehensives before but I thought it would tide me over until something nearer to home turned up. It never did and I ended up teaching Geography at St Aidan's for 25 extremely enjoyable years. It was a reminder again that there are certain key moments in life where important decisions can have a fundamental influence on the rest of your life. But I am glad to say that I have never regretted making this difficult choice.

St Aidan's was a fine place to work and the atmosphere amongst the staff was great, with all sorts of good-natured trouble-making and practical jokes being played between individuals. I worked under four different head teachers, all of whom I admired in different ways. Then after a few years I had to make another very important decision.

My Head of Department, Joyce, had been away from the school on two separate occasions looking after her newly born children. While she was away I had been acting as Head of the Department in her place. I had always assumed that, at some time in the future, I would like to be fully in charge of my own little empire. So when Joyce decided that she needed to retire properly in order to care for her two youngsters, I had the perfect opportunity to step into her shoes.

However, to my great surprise, I found myself uneasy about applying for the job. I became convinced that God was telling me not to apply. It wasn't easy, I admit, but I managed to stick to my instinct and so did not put my name forward. At the interview, a Geordie called John Rutter was appointed and I'm very pleased to say that he made an excellent department leader; he and I became firm friends as well as work colleagues.

What made my decision especially interesting was that, a short time later, the new head teacher, Jim Foster, offered me the chance to be the School's Chapel and Charity organiser. This meant I was responsible for planning the School's assemblies and for co-ordinating all the School's charity work.

As co-ordinator of the School assemblies it was my responsibility to prepare the programme of topics as well as to join the leaders' rota. Experience of leading worship at St Mark's Church in York was clearly an advantage (see Episode 8). However, I never found it easy preparing material but I felt the time given to preparation was very important.

Let me tell you about one assembly I took just before the summer holidays one year. I had adopted the practice of using the last assembly of the school year to challenge the students to try to do something different during the long summer holidays. It did not need to be anything expensive; in fact, better if it weren't; but the opportunity to try something new was a chance to discover talents and gifts that God had given us but which we had not yet used. I used as my personal example the plan I had for my next building project – the construction of a carport – an open-sided covering next to the house designed to protect the car. This would be by far my most demanding summer project so far. The story went something like this.

The Carport

Five years ago, my wife Nancy said to me: 'Darling, have you ever thought about building a carport? I feel so sorry for your car standing out on the driveway, getting more and more rusty from the rain while my car is nice and warm and dry and snug inside the garage.'

'No!' I declared firmly. 'We're not worshipping idols – a car's just a painted metal box with bits inside! Anyway, all cars will get rusty sooner or later and then have to go to the scrap yard and get broken up.'

Four years ago, my wife Nancy said to me: 'Sweetheart, have you ever thought about building a carport? All our neighbours have carports; Doreen and Brian next door, Les and Janet on the other side; John and Pat over the road. If we had one, too, it would mean we weren't looking like the poor, odd family out.'

'No!' I replied firmly. 'We're not having our lives ruled by what other people say and how they live their lives. We're our own people living our own lives.'

Three years ago, my wife Nancy said to me: 'Chunky Hunk, have you ever thought about building a carport? I worry about you in the cold, icy, snowy winter mornings. You have to go out in the freezing cold and scrape off all the snow and ice from the car before you can even start the long drive to work in Harrogate. A carport would be such a help.'

'No!' I said firmly. 'A little vigorous exercise first thing in the morning never did anybody any harm. That's the trouble with people today; they want life all too easy!'

Two years ago, my wife Nancy said to me: 'Dearest, have you ever thought about building a carport? I've been wondering; you know how house prices have suddenly started to shoot up? Well, if we built a carport, we'd increase the value of our property quite a bit. Think of our children. I know it's a long time in the future, but when we die they would have something better to inherit.'

'No!' I retorted indignantly. 'We're not having our lives ruled by trying to make more and more money. We'll be satisfied with what we have already. There are far more important things in life than chasing after money!'

Earlier this year, we went on holiday to the Lake District. We drove the car up to the cottage where we were staying and suddenly, there it was, a superbly built wooden carport with climbing plants entwined all around the framework. 'There it is!' I exclaimed in amazement, 'the carport of my dreams! I'll build one like that straight away when we get home!'

'What?!' said Nancy in mock alarm. 'You'll never be able to build anything so complicated as that, surely? It takes real skill you know.'

'Yes, I can,' I replied with all the enthusiasm of a new convert. 'I'll build it this summer – just you see.'

And so, after five years of Nancy's dogged persuasion, and convinced it was all my own idea, I finally took up the challenge. I first had to go through all the business of planning permission, building regulations and drainage approval but all that went well. Then, in the summer, the carport was all completed. I have to admit, I was quietly quite proud of my efforts. Just then Dave Wilson, one of the Design-Technology teaching staff from St Aidan's, happened to be passing by. He stopped to admire my wonderful creation. He studied it carefully for a moment, made a quick professional assessment and then declared 'Mmmm not bad, John. We always encourage the children to do a mock-up version beforehand!' Amazingly, Dave and I are still friends.

At least some of the staff must have been listening to the Assembly because it earned me the nickname of Johnny Carport.

Stories

There are scores of memorable St Aidan's stories I could relate but I'll have to restrict myself to just a couple. But first, a reminder of how in 1989 I shaved off my beard for a Christian Aid charity event. This was the first time Nancy had seen me unmasked. She was genuinely shocked but at least she had the

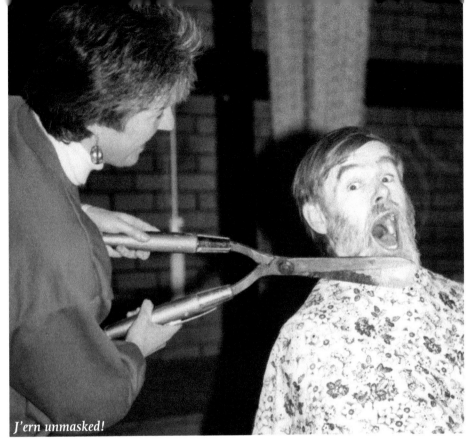

J'ern unmasked!

trauma slightly reduced by watching the action as it went on. Not so the four offspring who were speechless when they arrived home from school.

Now let me tell you about **Tim Pocock**. Tim had been a journalist on a provincial newspaper before entering teaching, so he had a good grasp of language. He was enthusiastically involved with all the sponsored charity events that I organised and I persuaded him to put his name to the forewords of the early walking books I produced.

Tim was also a keen footballer and wrote the weekly 'fanzine' magazine for Carlisle United, going regularly across the Pennines to watch his team. (A 'fanzine' is an amateur magazine produced by supporters as an alternative foil to the official club magazine.) When he came to St Aidan's, he formed a staff football team that he named Athletico Aidans and produced a fanzine every time the team played against another school staff team. It was really quite a prodigious workload but Tim took it all in his stride. I could only play for the team a couple of times because on Friday nights I was involved with leading the St Mark's Church youth group in York. However, when the time came for me to leave St Aidan's, Tim arranged a special testimonial match for me which included the production of a special fanzine. But not only that, Tim had contacted Everton FC and arranged for the Manager of the club to send a special certificate of commendation. I confess I was highly impressed.

Another larger than life figure was **Steve Hatcher**, the deputy head teacher for much of my time at St Aidan's. Apart from the fact that he was a passionate Liverpool supporter, we had several things in common; he was a Geographer, a sports fanatic and he had a seemingly insatiable desire to 'do a new project' every year. Dennis Richards, the head teacher, gave Steve carte blanche to do whatever building project in the school that he fancied, so each new school year would see the unveiling of some new teaching block or other.

The school intake had grown considerably while I was there and there was a lack of large spaces suitable for use during examination times as well as for other big events. Steve hit on the idea of extending an existing hall into a new dual-purpose facility which would serve as the school's new chapel but which could be used for other non-religious purposes as well. It was a huge undertaking but Steve relished the challenge.

When the time came for the official opening service of the new chapel, the chaplain, Wendy Wilby, recognising the enormous contribution Steve had made to the building, asked him if he would like to deliver the main Bible reading. The theme of the service was 'Unless the Lord build the house, they labour in vain that build it' (Psalm 127). I can't be certain if Wendy told Steve beforehand or not what the reading would be, but Steve felt honoured to be asked and so agreed. The passage in question was from 2 Chronicles 6 where King Solomon, surveying the magnificent Temple he had just finished building, prayed the following prayer: 'O God ... not even all heaven is large enough to hold you, so how can this Temple that I have built be large enough?' Smiles widened on the faces of the staff, there was a twinkle in Wendy's eye but Steve kept his cool.

I suppose I sought to say something about the **Geography** teaching I did, after all that's what I was being paid for. The Geography department was a happy and stable one with three of us, John Rutter, Janet Coatman and myself working for some 20 years or so together.

One of the attractions of teaching Geography was that students, when having to choose which subjects they should take, could always be offered the carrot of going away on field trips. Older readers may remember the 'Janet and John go on a picnic/ramble/holiday' series of Ladybird children's books that helped youngsters with their early reading. Well, we were the 'Janet and John (and John) team that went on a field trip'. In fact, we went on many field trips and I can honestly say I never became bored with going back to Langdale in the Lake District, Malham in North Yorkshire or Flamborough on the East Yorkshire coast. Indeed, I even agreed with my wife that we should retire to Flamborough, so inspiring is its landscape.

I mentioned earlier that I had first been enchanted with Langdale when I was completing my Scout Senior Explorer Badge in 1960 and my love for the place never died. When I eventually left St Aidan's the Geography department presented me with a fine water colour painting of the Langdale Pikes as a memento of happy days.

After having been working part-time for my last two years, by 2001 I was fully retired. For this special occasion, Tanya gave me a lovely present. It was a book she had written herself especially for the moment. It was titled 'Dad's Cookbook: the Essential Guide to Cooking during Retirement'. 'What a kind, thoughtful gesture from my dear daughter,' I thought. Then I opened it and started to read. There are recipes for all sorts of delights: how to make toast, how to make a pot of tea, how to eat a packet of chocolate biscuits without anyone finding out. But my favourite is probably the first in the book and one that I was certain I would need in the future. This first recipe is for how to make a 'Jam Butty'. Here it is.

INGREDIENTS
You will need:
Half a loaf of bread (at least)
Margarine
Very, very large pot of jam
Knife

This recipe works to best effect when just woken up, either mid-morning, mid-afternoon, mid-evening or at 3.00 am when you've just woken up due to too many snoozes during the previous day.

(1) Ensure the wife/family are otherwise engaged

(2) Spread margarine over slice of bread

(3) Spread jam on to margarine, very thickly. (This is crucial because, if anyone else was watching – which they aren't as you've already checked – they would think the jam was enough for four slices)

(4) Fold one sticky, jammy half of bread over on to the other half, making sure some oozes out on to your fingers

(5) Lick fingers clean of jam

(6) Force sandwich into mouth very quickly in case wife/kids should happen to appear suddenly

(7) Eat butty

(8) Repeat steps 1-7 with rest of the bread

I think this retirement present deserves a really big Star on the Star Chart; but what colour should it be?

EPISODE 7
St Aidan's Sponsored Charity Runs

Being Chair of the Charity Committee allowed me a virtually free rein to develop the role and this was how the interest in the sponsored charity runs and the production of the walking books developed. If I had accepted the Head of Geography department post, I don't think I would have had the time to concentrate on the book writing which became such an absorbing and enjoyable enterprise for me.

So had all this been part of God's long term plan for me when he guided me not to go for the Head of Geography post? I suspect it was.

What I think of as 'The Early Experiments' were the sponsored runs I arranged for each of the five years from 1994 to 1998. The first was the **1994 York Half Marathon**.

The Archbishop of Canterbury had launched an appeal for those suffering from the long civil war in Southern Sudan and because of my long-standing interest in the Sudan I felt I should take up the Archbishop's challenge. So I managed to persuade 12 of the staff at St Aidan's to take part in the 'Yorkie' Half Marathon race in the spring. What was especially encouraging was that six of the team had never run more than half that distance before. Everything went extremely well and we raised £2,500 in sponsorship for the Sudan. Although not a large amount by some standards, we were all delighted with the effort, especially as so many had been involved. And it laid the foundation for the following years' sponsored events.

I must at the outset say what tremendous support I had from St Aidan's Headteacher, Dennis Richards, who gave me great personal encouragement and, even more importantly, got the staff to be so highly motivated. That support was fully maintained in later years when the walking books came to be written.

1995 · Dales Way Relay

During the Spring half-term in 1994 Nancy and I had walked the Dales Way with Tanya and Sharon. From my point of view, it was a valuable experience in encouraging me to repeat the walk the following year (1995) as a School staff sponsored event. However, this time we would run the Dales Way as a relay and we would be sponsored for cancer research. I managed to get 18 staff 'volunteers', plus a number of their husbands and wives, to take part doing either five or 10 mile legs and the day went extremely well. It would all be good preparation for the following year. And so the tradition had been established.

As I have been reading through the documents that I have kept of all the staff relays that I organised, I'm reminded of how the staff responded so brilliantly to all my mad-cap ideas. It was this sense of camaraderie that made St Aidan's such a special place to work.

1996 · Tidewater Way – a Race of Two Halves

When we had walked the Dales Way in 1994 we had bumped into Tony Rablen who, a few years before, had been our curate in Rawcliffe. He told me he was preparing to write an alternative Coast to Coast walking guide that went from tidewater on the River Lune at Lancaster to tidewater on the River Wharfe at Ulleskelf near York. It was a 90 mile route of peaceful and scenic footpaths through the Lancashire and Yorkshire Dales. In 1994 Tony had completed the crossing, with slight variations to allow road walking through the night, in less than 24 hours. What he suggested was that I might like to check some of the route for him before he published the guidebook. What an offer!

I jumped at the opportunity, did some of the walk sections with him and then checked the rest of the route with Nancy. So in 1996 'Tidewater Way' came into existence after Tony had enlisted the wonderful cartographic skills of Mark Comer in producing the guidebook. Tony was kind enough to give generous acknowledgement of the support we had given him. But he need not have troubled himself, I'd become hooked.

Tony enthusiastically agreed when I broached the idea of inaugurating the walk with a sponsored relay run to be completed by the staff and a few friends at St Aidan's. All monies raised would be donated to Christian Aid. It sounded a bit quirky but the staff were used to me by this time and willingly agreed to take part. We decided to make it a 'Race of Two Halves' (reflecting the football catchphrase of a 'Game of Two Halves'). The Westies, comprising those born west of the Pennines, would run west to east while the Easties, born east of the Pennines, would go east to west. Progress was to be monitored by Joy Rice, anchored at base in Harrogate and feeding regular updates to Simon Stanley at Radio York. Tim Pocock produced a special 'Race of Two Halves Fanzine'. Apart from the Easties lead runner taking a wrong turn after the first 100 yards and then later going twice around Thorpe Arch prison, and one of the Geography teachers (not me!) getting lost, it was all a great success.

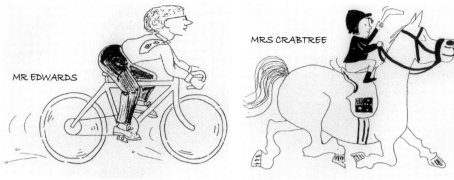

MR EDWARDS

MRS CRABTREE

1997 · Nidd Valley Challenge

MR HATCHER

The next year I organised a 24 hour, 100 mile staff relay that we called the **Nidd Valley Challenge**. Again it was to be a sponsored event for Christian Aid. This run – well, it started as a run idea – had the advantage that it passed close to Harrogate and there was already in existence 'The Nidd Valley Way', by Ken Piggin, which covered the central part of the Nidd Valley. I planned a route to cover the whole valley, from the source of the river on the slopes of Great Whernside (not to be confused with 'Whernside' which is a different mountain altogether) which would then join with Ken's route to Hampsthwaite. From there we would use the Nidd Valley Link and carry on to the Minster in York. However, by popular demand of the staff, my idea of just running the route was overruled and, instead, we made it not just a run or walk relay but 'a multi-mode locomotion relay'.* This meant that, as well

MRS WEHRING

as runners and walkers, we had different staff completing their sections on bikes, in canoes, in rowing boats, on horseback and, perhaps most memorable of all, on roller skates. As you can imagine, this made the organisation more complicated but it turned out to be well worth the effort. Dan Savage, a greatly talented Year 9 artist in the School, drew some wonderful staff cartoons of those taking part. We shall meet Dan later in Episode 9. It was a brilliant day and I was very pleased that I'd listened to the advice of those who'd suggested making it different.

Cartoons by Dan Savage

68

This was the same year that the School was celebrating the opening of the new chapel and so, a central feature of the relay route was that along the way we would visit 26 places of Christian worship, each one beginning with a different letter of the alphabet. This meant starting at 3.00am at the Zouche Chapel at York Minster and finishing at the new school chapel at St Aidan's. Finding a place for 'X' proved a little difficult but we compromised by saying that 'X' marked the cave where St Robert of Knaresborough had prayed and lived his hermit's life. Basing the idea on Robert Browning's poem 'How they brought the Good News from Ghent to Aix' we described our relay as 'How we brought the Good News from Zouche to Aidans'.

Nancy reminds me that it was her original idea and not mine to offer this as an option to the staff. My wife had the right idea yet again!

1998 · Whitby Way

The following year saw us inaugurate yet another new long distance walk. This time it was the **'Whitby Way'** which had been written by another friend, Leslie Stanbridge, who was the Archdeacon of York and a keen walker himself. It was designed as a sixty-six mile pilgrimage walk from York Minster across the North York Moors to Whitby Abbey. On the way the route visits Byland Abbey, Rievaulx Abbey and the site of Rosedale Abbey as well as St Gregory's Minster in Kirkdale and Lastingham Church with its unforgettable 1078 crypt.

Leslie was a cyclist as well as a walker and his guide book includes route information for cyclists in addition to directions for walkers.

2001 · Rezzy Rush

The foot-and-mouth outbreak of 2001 quickly spread across the UK. The highly infectious disease, which mainly affected cattle, pigs, sheep and goats, plunged the agricultural industry into its worst crisis for decades. From our own selfish point of view, this meant that we were unable to hold the April staff relay that I had planned because large areas of the countryside became prohibited to walkers. However, in order to keep the record straight, I think it is worth noting what we had prepared – Rezzy Rush.

Starting and finishing at the Harrogate Valley Gardens, this is a 40-mile trail visiting 10 local reservoirs. It can be used, if required, as a relay race between two teams, one going clockwise and the other anti-clockwise round the circuit. It is available as a free download from the LDWA website.

What made this trail different from the previous ones was that it incorporated a quasi-scientific emphasis as walkers were offered the opportunity to investigate the lifestyle of *Rezzysaurus regina*. The origin of this creature in Yorkshire waters is conjectural but it has been suggested that it first arrived sometime in the 14th century at the time when bands of marauding Scotsmen

Cartoon by Nancy

New stepping stones:
How convenient!

were laying waste to this part of Yorkshire. There is an intriguing possibility that in the pandemonium of ferocious armed conflict the pair of Scottish mascots, taken with the Scots on their southern forays, escaped into the local waters.

Over the centuries there have been numerous reported sightings, unfortunately all unconfirmed it must be admitted, of one of nature's most fascinating creatures. All new information is being collated at the Loof Lirpa Publications office in Harrogate. Let the reader understand.

EPISODE 8
Church and New Zealand

Having been a **Lay Reader** in Jamaica, I offered to do the same work in the UK but this first involved going through a pretty rigorous training course before I could qualify. After I obtained my licence, Robin Fletcher, our Vicar, asked me if I would consider acting as 'the permanent face' leading the Family Worship services at St Mark's Church in Rawcliffe, just up the road from where we were living in Howard Drive. With some trepidation I agreed and soon found the work very satisfying.

St Mark's is essentially what is sometimes called a 'Teaching Church' where explaining the faith is prioritised in a way that is not always as central in other churches. We took our four youngsters with us because there was good provision for the children's teaching. I like to think they received a good grounding in the basics of the Christian faith.

It was a flourishing congregation and we used a clicker counter to record our numbers. Our young son Peter was doing the counting one Sunday and came up to me looking very jubilant, just as I was about to start the service. 'Dad,' he exclaimed excitedly and clearly oblivious of the irony, 'we're a hundred – dead!'

Whilst at St Mark's, I helped Sylvia Mutch as assistant, and then became leader of the Pathfinder Group. This was very rewarding but not always easy. A friend summed up the situation when he remarked 'Boys will be boys ... and so will the girls sometimes!'

Nevertheless, it was a great place to bring up our young brood. Robin arranged Church family hikes for most bank holidays and there was an annual house party weekend away. Every New Year's Eve, Robin and his wife Sheila would open their home to all church members for a New Year party. All these events were family oriented and our youngsters got to mix with others of their own age. Above all, they were tremendous fun.

We made some life-long friends at St Mark's. For example, Harold and Celia Rutt, with their children Jill and Martin, became Godparents to our children and would regularly come for Sunday lunch when we would all feast sumptuously on ... wait for it ... beans on toast.

Nancy has said on several occasions how much she valued the Church. It acted as a lifeline for her while I was away working in Harrogate and she had the four children to look after. It also provided her with the opportunity to begin a mid-week Toddler Service for other young Mums and their infants. From this experience she would go on to offer herself for ordination, first as a deacon and then later as priest.

1994 was a memorable year in several respects. The highlight was in May when **Nancy was ordained as a priest** in York Minster. She worked half-time in Clifton Parish, with special responsibility for developing a congregation on the neighbouring Clifton Moor, a former Second World War airfield site, where a whole new residential, commercial and leisure development was taking place. At first this meant holding services in the new Primary School, with all the attendant hassle of moving furniture before and after the services.

This was followed shortly by Sharon's confirmation in July when she became a member of both the Anglican and the Methodist Churches.

Then a couple of years later, in 1997, Nancy received some exciting news. It was the confirmation of the go-ahead to erect a **new church building on Clifton Moor**. This was to be a joint Ecumenical Anglican-Methodist venture and she got on extremely well with her Methodist counterpart. The Church was designed as a dual-purpose Church and Community Centre as there had been no plans drawn up for the latter facility. Everyone seemed satisfied with this, the churches especially, because it meant that we could obtain council funding towards the project. The new building was opened in 1998, the same year as Robin Fletcher retired as Vicar of Clifton. By this time Nancy was thinking of moving herself to become a Vicar of her own parish.

In **1999** Nancy was offered and accepted the post of Vicar of Heslington, the University parish on the south-east edge of York. The move from Rawcliffe would take place in the New Year. This, like Clifton Moor, was a joint Anglican-Methodist Church so her experience stood her in good stead. The church selectors were even more pleased when they learned that I was willing to join the team as a Lay Reader.

Nancy took up her appointment in the spring of 2000. We rented out our house in Rawcliffe and moved to the Vicarage in Heslington in time for Easter. Let's say our new home was on the big side; never again would we be able to say that we were a four-toilet family.

Nancy had vowed, above all else, that she would tread carefully when we first arrived at Heslington. She did, however, persuade me to dig a pond in the vicarage garden. Accordingly, I excavated a large hole but before I could fill it with water the recipe said 'Line the pond first with an old carpet before laying the pond liner' (this is to avoid any sharp stones piercing the plastic and causing leakage). Buying the liner was easy but getting an old carpet was a little troublesome. Until, that is, the new vicar came across a piece just the right size hiding away in a disused alcove hidden behind a curtain in the church. 'This will do fine,' she said and accordingly I put it in the bottom of the hole. Once the liner was laid down I started the tap running. A few days later the vicar's Methodist colleague returned from holiday and began making enquiries about the whereabouts of the students' special Friday night prayer mat .....

Heslington had had a very popular community bonfire-fireworks event for 30-odd years and I took on the job of managing it when we first arrived. After a few years in the role, I was suddenly swamped with the mass of public liability-risk assessment paperwork that we had so far avoided. In retrospect, I imagine that we ought to have been completing it for all the previous years but I admit to losing a few nights' sleep in what I can only imagine comes under the general name of 'stress'. Happily, everything 'on the night' went off well. However, the Church realised how fortunate it had been in never having had any misfortunes and decided, rightly, that it could no longer risk breaking 'health and safety' regulations no matter how irksome they might have seemed to some people. So that was the end of the bonfire and fireworks.

I had much less stress with the Walking Group that I organised and our regular band of Ruth, Peter, John and Sue were joined by others as I 'persuaded' them to help me with the reccying of walks for some of the walking books I was preparing. Their faithful fellowship and good humour were greatly appreciated.

At Heslington, I became responsible for co-ordinating the children's and youth work. This involved going into the two Primary Schools to lead assemblies and I relished this. I had had secondary school teaching experience but speaking to primary age children was altogether different. You would ask for a volunteer and immediately the whole assembly would want to join in! It was hugely enjoyable.

Heslington Church Summer Club

73

We built on this good relationship by inviting the youngsters to come to the Kids' Summer Club each year. These were hilarious good fun, with some Christian teaching incorporated, I ought to point out, and I was favoured by a terrific supporting team who more or less did everything I asked of them.

The third strand in the children's work was the 5-a-Side Inter-Church Football tournaments I arranged. There were about half a dozen churches that took part, some fielding more than one team. On each tournament day every team played all of the others in a 'round robin' arrangement. Winners held the trophy until the following term when we next played.

At this point, it's worth mentioning a book I somehow came across called 'Thank God for Football' by Peter Lupson. In the mid-1990s Peter had started a church football league on Merseyside for boys in their early teens. However, he soon became aware that some of the lads were ridiculed by their friends for playing in a church league. Then Peter read that a Merseyside church, St Domingo's Chapel, had been the cradle of both Everton FC and Liverpool FC. His discovery led Peter to research further, how many other clubs of church origin could he find? His finding was quite extraordinary. He discovered that 12 out of the 38 clubs that have played in the English Premier League since its inception in the 1992-93 season can trace their origin directly to a church.* Yet a good number of these clubs knew little about their origins or founders.

Reading Peter's book made me feel that the Heslington Church Football Trophy was following in a noble tradition, even if it was on an entirely different scale.

In January **2007** Nancy was given ten weeks' sabbatical leave and at last we were able to take up the long-standing offer from my sister Maureen and her husband Bill to visit them in **New Zealand**. Naturally we spent some time with them at their orchard in North Island. I had thought that when Bill had retired from his job as an industrial chemist and taken up a smallholding, it was a sort of glorified allotment-relaxation venture he had embarked on. No such thing! It was a highly organised commercial undertaking, making full use of Bill's chemical engineering background in the use of fertilisers, insecticides and marketing techniques.

Maureen gave us the loan of her car and this meant that we had a terrific time touring around both North and South Islands. In NZ they drive on the proper side of the road, use sensible money and speak good English, so we had minimal problems. NZ, of course, is full of Geography and I was pleasantly surprised to find that much of what I had taught scores of students 30-odd years before proved to be reasonably true. One thing, though, that I

---

* *The 12 clubs are Aston Villa, Barnsley, Birmingham City, Bolton Wanderers, Everton, Fulham, Liverpool, Manchester City, Queens Park Rangers, Southampton, Swindon Town and Tottenham Hotspur.*

Mitre Peak at Milford Sound

had not appreciated is that the capital, Wellington, sits bang on top of the major Pacific Rim fault-line, rather like San Francisco lies astride the San Andreas fault complex.

Highlights of the visit included glacier-bagging, and trips to the fiords at Milford Sound and Doubtful Sound. We are constantly amazed at how the advertising industry can persuade people to part with their money on unpromising products. According to the Visitor Centre, Milford Sound boasts up to 8,000 mm (yes, 8 metres) of rain a year* but in spite of this visitors go in their thousands. (The day we went, I should add, there was brilliant sunshine.)

Maureen and Bill

Panning for gold ('We **guarantee** you will take home some gold dust' said the blurb) was great fun. What happens is that the company buys in gold dust, mixes it with gravel and then teaches you how to separate it by panning. And it works every time; we brought home our samples to prove it. Nancy went swimming with dolphins; we were intrigued by Puzzle World; we walked both the Tongariro Crossing (featured in 'Lord of the Rings') and the Abel Tasman Trail and we had a great time on a wine-tasting bike-tour of the Marlborough vineyards. I suppose you could say that we have been permanently hooked by the advertisers. We will now drink virtually no wine unless it bears the 'Sauvignon Blanc – New Zealand' label.

Towards the end of **2010** we started making preparations for leaving Heslington Vicarage because Nancy had told the Church wardens that she would be retiring after Christmas. We had had an exceptionally happy time and were both very conscious of how much we would miss the Church and everything that went on at Heslington.

Nancy, therefore, went ahead with the downsizing operations. You have probably realised by now that Nancy is basically a thrower-out whilst I am essentially a 'keep-it-in-case-it-comes-in-useful' sort of guy. Finding a workable compromise has been a good test of our compatibility. At first, I

Puzzle World – the leaning Tower of Wanaka

coped reasonably well with seeing so much of my 'good wood' thrown unceremoniously out of the garage and given to 'good homes' but when, quelle horreur, some was actually banished to the dump, I could have done with stress counselling.

Christmas will remain an exceptionally memorable time. The Minster Carol Service, which included tap-dancing in the nave, would be Nancy's last time as Chaplain to Archbishop Holgate's School; it was the last Christmas Concert with Badger Hill School, who showered both of us with gifts; our last Christmas services at Heslington and the last Christmas with all the family packed into the Vicarage for Christmas dinner.

Her actual last service was at 11.00 am on 11.01.11 – the Blessing of sister Kathy and new husband John's Wedding. Sadly, it was time to move on. It had been a wonderful eleven years.

In 2011 we set ourselves the target of walking LEJOG in five months (see Episode 10). After we had completed the walk we started settling in at Flamborough and I joined the team responsible for children's work. It wasn't long before Nancy was asked to 'look after' a church in Filey, and then one in Scarborough while they were waiting for a new Vicar. Then in 2015 she agreed to be the 'Permanent Face' at Bempton Church, a couple of miles up the road from Flamborough and one of the four churches in our Benefice grouping. As with all the other churches with which we have been associated, we are extremely grateful for the welcome we have been given. The congregation is most friendly, there's a full social calendar and the renowned Pudding Club does sterling work for charity.

*I checked this figure on the Internet and Wikipedia reports that the **average** rainfall is a mere 6,412 mm (252 inches) per year. Nevertheless, the **record** highest annual total was 9,259 mm (364 inches) in 2016.*

EPISODE 9
Christian Aid and the Books

I first became interested in overseas development work when I was in the Sixth Form at Waterloo Grammar and I organised the Oxfam Pledged Gifts scheme, persuading students to make regular donations to help different Oxfam projects.

It is probably not too much to say that my passion for development work can be said to have been motivated from a single word that I saw on a Christmas poster appeal aimed at helping refugees and others in great poverty. The poster had the easily recognisable Christmas picture of Mary and Joseph travelling by donkey towards Bethlehem.

What was striking about the picture, however, was that there was only one word written. That word was **'Inasmuch'**. That's all it said. Yet it spoke volumes. Fifty-odd years ago people in our country had a better knowledge of their Bibles and they would have recognised this very unusual word from the King James Authorised Version of the Bible as referring to the Parable of

Inasmuch ...

78

the Sheep and the Goats told by Jesus and recorded in Matthew's Gospel, Chapter 25. In the parable Jesus says 'Inasmuch as...you have fed the hungry, given water to the thirsty, welcomed strangers, clothed the naked, cared for the sick or visited those in prison, *then you did it for me!*'

It was just one word, 'Inasmuch' but it had a very important influence on my life.

The decision to support Christian Aid came after I had returned from the Sudan because the Church in Prestwich had links with the charity. What I had not known at that time was that Christian Aid had been involved in the initial establishment of VSO. In my own simple way, I argued that if Jesus told his followers to help the poor, then we should just get on and do so. I thought that Christian Aid was one practical way the churches could counter some of the negative publicity they sometimes received. Many people outside the churches thought helping the world's poorest communities was 'a good idea', so the churches might as well benefit from that goodwill. I particularly liked the strap line that Christian Aid came to use when it declared 'We Believe in Life Before Death' – a clever slogan that proclaimed the Christian social message without being too churchy. In fact, Christian Aid goes out of its way to stress that it is not a missionary body. It classes as a charity and is the official relief and development agency of 41 different church denominations in the UK and Ireland and works to support sustainable development, stop poverty, support civil society and provide disaster relief in poor communities throughout the world.

At first I was just involved with activities during Christian Aid Week in May of each year. More active involvement came after we returned from Jamaica and settled down in York. I soon found that I actually *enjoyed*

The Christian Aid Shop

Courtesy of Evening Press

No, no, no! Don't be silly. I'm selling the thing; not playing it!

'doing Christian Aid' – it was not a great chore, rather it was great fun, especially the Christian Aid 'Shop' which was a glorified jumble sale held in a redundant church in the middle of York each year.

But there was an important ethical/moral consideration to be held in mind. Why was I doing it? I constantly had to remind myself that I wasn't doing it just for enjoyment. The whole purpose of the work was to raise money to save people's lives – it was not, in other words, just to satisfy my personal need for fulfilment. On the other hand, showing that you enjoyed the work meant other people were more likely to be persuaded to join in.

For a number of years I served on the York Christian Aid Committee and then I was invited to become Chair of the group. Much later, when we moved home to live at Flamborough, I became Chair of the Bridlington Group as well as becoming an official Christian Aid Volunteer. This meant I had official accreditation to go into Schools to take assemblies and teach lessons if required. This proved to be a delightful experience, primary school youngsters being far less inhibited than their secondary school counterparts.

However, that is jumping ahead; it was becoming Chair of the York Group which was the important step. Apart from anything else, the Secretary of the group was Mark Comer and he was quickly to become the indispensable cartographic and artistic presenter of the walking books which were about to come on stream. There is not a shadow of doubt that without Mark's brilliant expertise and support, the books could not have materialised in the form they did.

And that brings me conveniently on to 'The Books'. I could equally well have put this following section into the Work and School compartment because St Aidan's was so much involved and because the books followed on logically from the early experiments with the sponsored runs and walks. However, I felt that putting them under the Christian Aid umbrella would emphasise that they were all being written specifically for Christian Aid.

The Books

Nancy and I had enjoyed walking ever since we got married in 1972. In that year, soon after our wedding, we climbed the Yorkshire Three Peaks. I had run the fell race several times but it was a major challenge for my new wife. I instigated the practice of using 'Persuasion' as a carrot to encourage my flagging spouse to keep going – 'You can have a bite of Mars bar at the top of the next slope'. It worked a treat and we remembered the trick years later when our youngsters were being dragged out walking (Tanya's description, not mine). In that same summer, we backpacked the recently opened 'Cleveland Way' National Trail in North Yorkshire. Then later on, when the children were growing up, we would try to combine beach holidays for them with some walking for ourselves. This meant that by the time came for the book writing to begin, we had a fair amount of walking already under our boots.

I made the decision at the outset that all profits would go to Christian Aid. The delight and satisfaction I derived from the experience was more than ample reward. Add to that, the fact that I was doing it for charity ought to have ensured that at least some of the copies would be sold!

Abbeys Amble (1999) was the first to be written.

You might have guessed that, since helping Tony Rablen with 'Tidewater Way', I'd been dreaming of creating my own walk and for most of 1998 I had been working on my first attempt. I was going to call it 'Abbeys Amble' and in 1999 it was printed. So began another chapter in my life, linked to what had gone before but distinct in its own right. I must say that a few years before, I would never have had the faintest idea that I would have been able to write a book myself. I was convinced that this was a gift from God. Numerous friends gave invaluable help, especially Nancy who took the photos and drew the cartoons*, and Mark Comer who prepared all the maps and manuscript for publication. David Casson, father of Alison whom I had taught, most generously took Nigel Bromhead up in his plane to take the aerial photographs while Dan Savage, whom we met in Episode 7, produced his magnificent line drawings.

Abbeys Amble describes a 103 miles circular route that starts and finishes at Ripon Cathedral. It links up three famous Yorkshire Abbeys (Fountains, Bolton Priory and Jervaulx) as well as visiting three Yorkshire castles (Ripley, Bolton and Middleham).

Here's the Foreword that Tony Rablen wrote for me:

'John Eckersley had a dream. It was a glorious dream; a noble dream; a happy dream. The gallant hero of the dream was none other than - John Eckersley. In the dream he was opening a book - it was the new handbook of the **Long Distance Walkers Association (LDWA)**, *containing an alphabetical compendium of all the long distance walks in the entire country. In the dream, the first walk in the book was Abbeys Amble, by - John Eckersley.'*

But it was not to be! The dream didn't come true; Abbeys Amble was pipped into second place in the alphabetical list by something called Abberley Amble, a gentle 20 mile stroll somewhere in Worcestershire.

Never mind; I managed to see the funny side and was delighted that the sales of the book went well. The staff at St Aidan's were brilliant in acting as agents selling the book at their churches and amongst their friends as well as taking

---

* *Nancy's cartoons of me must have been pretty accurate. She was leading a churches' training event some time after the publication and a selection of the books was on display. One lady, who did not know me from Adam, pointing to one of the drawings, reacted in amazement and declared: 'I saw this man in York the other day - is he your husband?!'*

part in the, by now traditional, inaugural relay which finished in the dark at Ripon Cathedral. My appetite for producing walking guides had been well and truly whetted and so the latter half of 1999 was spent furiously preparing for a second effort which would, hopefully, be printed in time for the 2,000 Millennium Celebrations.

John mused on the faithfulness with which farmers always site their gates in the muddiest parts of the field...

ECHOES or Eckoes? (2000)

Lists of the highest points of the different English Counties have been in existence for a long time but I managed to come up with a new name for these county tops – I decided to call them 'ECHOES' (an acronym for 'English Counties Highest Original or Engineered Summits'). An 'original summit' is a natural one which has not been greatly altered by human activity whereas an 'engineered summit' is one that humans have constructed. Examples of engineered summits include ancient hill-forts as well as raised, concrete-covered reservoirs. Nancy thought this sounded just a wee bit too serious. 'How about,' she mused, 'calling it ECKOES (Earnest Climbers Kiss on Every Summit)?' Remember my middle name?

Since the previous summer I had been preparing maps and text for a series of circular walks, each of which would include the highest point of an English county. Obviously, it involved travelling all over the country but, once again, it was hugely rewarding and I was surprised at how fortunate I was in being able to devise attractive walks for each county. Nancy accompanied me on a good number including the eight we bagged in just one week's holiday during the schools' autumn half-term. How we managed to cram so much into such a short time remains a small miracle.

There was a lot of pressure to have the book published before May in time for Christian Aid Week. But we managed it. The plan was then to get 'volunteers' to co-ordinate walks to the tops of each of the 40 counties *and all to do it at the same time on Sunday 7 May 2000*. Don Savage, my artist Daniel's father, took a hired van and toured the country beforehand to drop off copies of the book to those schools that were taking part.

Amazingly, I got the volunteers and, except for Kent, every one of the 40 summits was bagged. It was ironic that Kent missed out because its ECHOES lies just a couple of hundred metres off the main road and so could be easily reached. However, an electrical storm made that team pull out. A pity, but the overall event was judged to have been a great success.

Exploring Lake Pickering (2003)

In 2003 a third book came on stream. In 1902 Percy Kendall had described how a great lake, Lake Pickering, had existed in the Vale of Pickering during the Ice Age. 'Exploring Lake Pickering' was a belated centennial tribute to Percy Kendall. His original ideas have since been modified but recent investigations have confirmed that a lake did exist, although smaller than at first thought. Moreover, other research has discovered that, immediately after the Ice Age, another separate lake, known as Lake Flixton, was formed in the eastern part of the Vale. The 'Lake Pickering Circuit' is a 155 mile trail following the higher ground around the edges of the two lakes. The trail is made up of 36 separate but inter-linked day circular walks, in the same way as Abbeys Amble had been devised, which pass along the Howardian and Tabular Hills, the North Sea coastal cliffs and the Yorkshire Wolds. The advantages of using inter-linked day circular walks is that there is no need to arrange overnight bed and breakfast; you don't need to carry heavy bags and, because you have not pre-booked accommodation, you can always cancel a day's walk if the weather is bad.

Helmsley Castle
(An example of David Casson's aerial photos)

The Vale of Pickering has a rich history of Christian witness going back at least to the 7th century and each of the walks is designed to include at least one place of Christian worship as well as places of natural beauty and secular interest, so one extra attraction of the trail is that it can be regarded as a pilgrimage walk.

Although it was now 18 months since I had retired from teaching at St Aidan's, I managed to persuade some of my former colleagues to come on another of 'John's Jolly Jaunts' (after all, it was for charity; and Christian Aid at that) in order to inaugurate the trail. It was not strictly speaking a relay as 'Abbeys Amble' had been; rather different individuals or groups each undertook to complete one of the 36 inter-linked circuits. So a total of 384 miles was covered on the launch day.

Cleveland Circles (2006)

By now, we were on a roll. For the previous few years, Nancy and I had tried to make a habit of going walking at least one day a week on Nancy's day off, which was usually a Friday. Rather than doing 'any old walk' we had tried to develop a sequence so that, for example, we would work through the different day circular walks that were part of a bigger, interconnected trail. We were now looking for a new project and Nancy suggested that we might re-visit the Cleveland Way and see if it was possible to devise a number of stand-alone day circuits that could be joined together to make up the Cleveland Way, the first long-distance National Trail we had walked after we had been married in 1972. At first I thought Nancy's idea was a bit far-fetched and over-optimistic but, being unable to make any better suggestion, I went along with the proposal. As so often, I had to admit that my wife was right after all and the project proved highly enjoyable. Of course, devising circular inter-linked walks means that you discover many delightful places away from the single line of the National Trail.

Rievaulx Abbey
(An example of
Dan Savage's line
drawings)

The Cleveland Way skirts the edge of the North York Moors National Park and traverses magnificent moorland and coastal countryside. 'Cleveland Circles' divides the 108-mile linear route into 30 separate, but inter-linked walks so that, like our previous walking guides, the whole trail can be covered over an extended period without the need to fix overnight accommodation.

Each day circuit is about ten miles long but includes options of about five miles for those preferring shorter routes. Once again, we tried to include historic churches and other places of worship in the routes so there is a pilgrimage flavour to the whole walk.

Nancy took virtually all the photos; Mark Comer did all the artistic layout of the guidebook and Dan Savage produced his inspiring line drawings. We launched the walk and accompanying guidebook for Christian Aid Week in May.

Wilberforce Way (2007)

Totally out of the blue, I had been asked the previous year, just when the Cleveland Circles project was virtually completed, if I would like to devise a walk for the 2007 William Wilberforce commemorations. I jumped at the chance. The remit was to develop a 60-mile route across the Yorkshire Wolds from Hull (where Wilberforce was born) through Pocklington (where he went to school) to York (where he became MP for the County of Yorkshire).

In 1788 Wilberforce introduced his first anti-slavery motion into Parliament. He would do the same for the next 18 years because the opposition to his campaign was so entrenched. Eventually in 1807 the House of Commons voted by an overwhelming majority to abolish the slave trade. So 2007 marked the 200th anniversary of the Act of Parliament abolishing British involvement in the Trans-Atlantic Slave Trade. This, however, was not the end of slavery itself in the British Empire; that had to wait until 1833. Then at last an estimated 800,000 men and women were set free. To placate the opposition, it was agreed that the plantation owners would receive £20 million compensation. William Wilberforce had given 53 years of his life to the abolition cause and he died just three days after seeing his efforts succeed.

Apart from a couple of places where the route follows tarred roads, the line of the walk was reasonably straightforward to devise and, as with the earlier books, we made it into a string of inter-connected circular walks. We continued to be surprised at the wealth of local history, almost on our doorstep, of which we had been unaware. As the research went on, we were able to focus on a number of additional locations that had special importance in the struggle for basic Human Rights.

Whitby Abbeylands (2008)

Around the 1990s, the Friends of Whitby Abbey had undertaken to devise a route around the boundaries of the Abbey estate as it had existed in medieval times. However, the plans for the circular route still lay in the Friends' in-tray until, in 2008, they asked Nancy and myself if we would be interested in offering some suggestions. We readily agreed and planned a set of 13 inter-linked circular walks which join together to trace the 53-mile boundary of the medieval lands owned by Whitby Abbey. I suggested the routes and Nancy took many of the photos. Roger Pickles, Chair of the Friends of the Abbey, researched and wrote all the historical information and all the production and marketing of the book was left for the Friends to arrange.

Whitby Abbey

One of the walks crosses an area of heather moorland on the North York Moors that had been devastated by fire a few years before. Yet ironically the fire had revealed scores of examples of prehistoric rock art, including 'cup and ring' marks, that had lain covered for perhaps millennia and of which the archaeologists had previously been unaware.

Stone crosses of various ages and varied uses – churchyard or preaching crosses, memorial crosses, waymarkers and even boundary markers – are a recurrent feature of the walks. Perhaps the most prominent is the Caedmon Cross at the head of the 199 Steps up to Whitby Abbey. It was carved in 1898 as a memorial to the 'father of English poetry'.

Alphabetting in East Yorkshire (2010)

Although we did not produce a new book in 2009, we took the opportunity to prepare 'Alphabetting in East Yorkshire'. We had conceived the idea of seeing if we could devise walks to some of Yorkshire's most outlandish sounding places – Ugglebarnby, Thorngumbald, Giggleswick, Wetwang and so on. However, the project narrowed itself down to finding walks that were confined to East Yorkshire and each of the 26 separate routes had to include a place or feature beginning with a different letter of the alphabet. As you might imagine, I had great delight poring over the maps and finding unlikely places for Q, U, V, X, Y and Z. But find them we did and we managed to get 26 different groups to trial the walks in the mid-summer of 2009. The trials went well and the book was published in 2010. Once again, we gave the profits to Christian Aid. In previous years we had supported some of Christian Aid's special partnership programmes in which all 'new money' raised by contributors is match-funded by the European Union. In the case of 'Alphabetting' the partnership project was a farming and water programme in Zimbabwe which was match-funded by an astonishing 9 to 1 by the EU. Clearly the EU trusts charities like Christian Aid to use its funds effectively rather than risk trusting potentially corrupt politicians.

Walking St Hilda's Way (2015)

John Eckersley was getting grumpy; all his brilliant ideas for another long walk in 2015 seemed to be getting nowhere. Then suddenly out of the blue, his wife Nancy was asked by Barry Pyke, the Vicar of Hinderwell, 'Our Whitby Deanery are wanting a project to celebrate 1400 years since the birth of our great northern saint, Hilda, in 614. Any ideas?'

Like greyhounds out of their traps, we were away: 'Great, when do we start?' we asked.

'It just so happened', as they say, that on our first visit to Barry's vicarage, Nancy spotted in the corner of his study (incredibly untidy, it has to be said) a dusty picture showing a resplendent icon image of St Hilda herself. Surrounding the saint were pictures illustrating important aspects of her work. The icon would make the perfect cover for the book and provide themes for each of the day walks. Nancy obtained the necessary permission for its use.

The result is St Hilda's Way, a new 40 miles long-distance trail in North Yorkshire, starting from St Hilda's Well in Hinderwell and finishing at Whitby where Hilda was once Prioress of Whitby Abbey. The walk is designed as a pilgrimage and visits eight Churches and Chapels all dedicated to St Hilda, as well as two other churches named after St Hedda and St Mary. At each location there is a different focus on one aspect of the saint's life and the opportunity for reflection and meditation.

The route crosses part of the North York Moors and then follows the line of the Esk Valley. We produced a guide-book but this time it was rather different from previous publications and the emphasis was primarily one of pilgrimage. Nancy took all the photos and wrote the special interest and prayer sections whilst I compiled the route descriptions.

'Walking St Hilda's Way' would be the last of the walking books. I am still amazed at the delight and enjoyment that Nancy and I have derived from producing them.

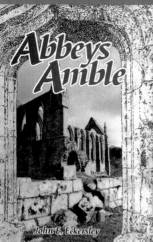

Abbeys Amble
John E. Eckersley

ECHOES
or Eckoes?
John E. Eckersley

Exploring Lake Pickering

Cleveland Circles

The Books

WILBERFORCE WAY
by John E. Eckersley
(incorporating Walking With Wilberforce)

Alphabeting
in East Yorkshire
John and Nancy Eckersley

WALKING St HILDA'S WAY
NANCY AND JOHN ECKERSLEY

Whitby Abbeylands Walks
13 linked circular walks around the boundary of the medieval estates of the medieval abbey of Whitby
John Eckersley & Roger Pickles
PUBLISHED BY
The Friends of Whitby Abbey

EPISODE 10
Walking Land's End to John o'Groats (LEJOG)

Explanation of the pacing shown on the map – I've used imperial units because both Nancy and I are getting on a bit now and we're not used to new-fangled things like metric.

The total distance on the route that we were taking was 1,280 miles. In 'old money' that means (1280 x 1760 x 3 x 12) inches. At a slow walking pace my average pace length is 30 inches while Nancy's is only 24 inches.

So for the whole walk I would take ((1280 x 1760 x 3 x 12) divided by 30) = 2,703,360 paces.

On the other hand, Nancy would take ((1280 x 1760 x 3 x 12) divided by 24) = 3,379,200 paces.

Nancy would be walking a lot more and expending much more energy than me, if you can believe this logic.

To set the scene, here is **The Fly on the Rucksack's Tale** (a conversation as overheard whilst being carried on David Maughan's 'North of England Way', April 2010).

J: It's hard to think that in a year's time you'll be retired, Love, and we'll have all the time in the world together. What do you fancy doing to celebrate?

N: I want to walk Land's End to John o'Groats.

J: 'What! That's an 'eck of a long way for a couple of old pensioners. Do you realise what it will involve? It's not just a gentle stroll, you know and, if I can say it kindly, you're not the spring chicken I fell for 40 years ago! (and, come to think of it, I don't suppose I'm the macho hunk you drooled over either.)

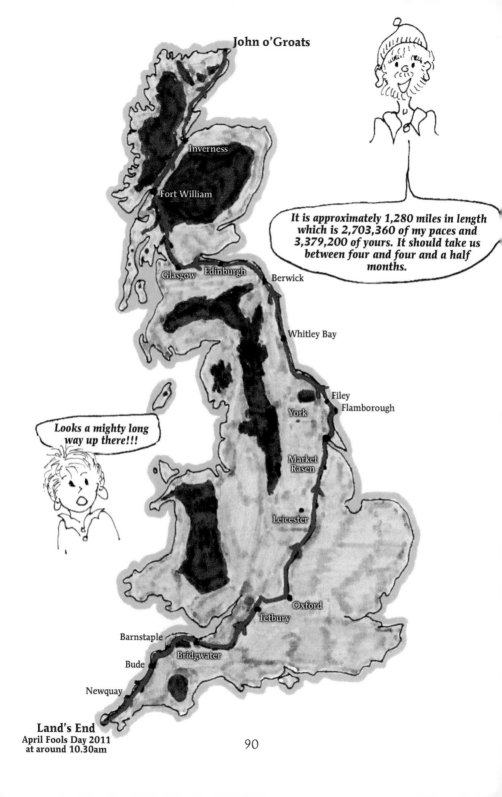

N: Well, if you want to wimp out you could always stay home and watch the telly.

J: Listen, for a start, some of it is pretty rugged country. What if we have an accident like a twisted ankle or take a wrong turn out on the hills just when it's getting dark and starting to rain? Can you imagine the papers: 'Two old codgers lost on the hills' – it doesn't bear thinking about.

N: But you don't have to take the high level route. Andrew McCloy's book suggests three possible routes and we could avoid the Pennine Way entirely if you felt frightened. Actually, I've been thinking about it for some time and, as I said, you don't have to come or perhaps you'd just like to choose the easier sections. Tell you what, I could do the walk and you could drive the support car, meet me every few miles, give me a hot drink and encouragement, then pick me up at the end and prepare the evening meal. You might want to take a book to read so you didn't get bored. That'd work, don't you think?

J: But then there's Scotland! Have you thought about that? All those midges, mosquitoes and clegs – with your allergies, you'd get eaten alive! And what about the food? Oats for breakfast, gruel for lunch and then haggis for supper – you'd never survive! And the rain – it never stops! Talk about raining cats and dogs, it's tigers and wolves up there! And your Mum. She's getting on now; what if anything happened to her while we were away?

N: We'd keep in contact through my sister Kathy. You could leave your semaphore flags at home and instead I'll take my high tech stuff – it's called a mobile phone – just in case.

J: I can think of another problem. What about our six grandkids, scattered over the rest of the country? They're probably hoping that they'll be able to see much more of us once you retire; they'll not expect us to be swanning off all over the place on a five month long holiday jaunt!'

N: Actually, what I had in mind was that we could plan our route so that we visited them all in the course of the walk, stayed with them for a few days and had some high quality time seeing them.

J: Then what about the morality? You know I'll feel guilty about the whole thing. How can we justify a five-month long, expensive, self-indulgent jolly when there's so much hardship in the world, so much suffering, so many people feeling the pinch in these times of financial hardship?

N: It's just possible we might get one or two people to sponsor us for Christian Aid. Would that salve your conscience? I'd say I was doing it all for fun and you could pretend to be earnest and say you were doing it all as a philanthropic gesture. And I'll tell you something else. We could get Phil to set up a blog on the website so that people could see what we were up to and could donate through the Just Giving Scheme. Anyway, I want to use the time to think, pray, reflect and try to discern what God's plan for the next stage of our lives might be.

J: Possibly ...

N: But there's one thing I am adamant about. This has got to be a once-in-a-lifetime romantic stroll – just you and me. No pressure; no hassle; and certainly – certainly there is no question whatsoever of the stress of writing another book! Scores of other people have already written about Land's End to John o'Groats. It would require an enormous amount of effort doing all the mapping, taking all the notes, doing all the research, snapping all the photos. I know you: you'd be so tired at the end of the day and you'd be lying awake all night wondering whether you've got the story right that it would all become a great burden instead of the holiday of a lifetime. So definitely – NO BOOK – not on this occasion.

J: 'Mmmm ... Nance, you know, I'm beginning to warm to the idea. Perhaps 'Land's End to John o'Groats' isn't such a bad suggestion after all ... When would you like to start?

N: How about All Fools' Day, 1st April 2011?'

So the walk had been publicised as starting on All Fools' Day but as the last niceties of house purchasing had not been finalised we had to put our furniture in store, with a wonderfully obliging Mother-in-law and Sister-in-law offering garage and house space, and so we set off, literally, 'of no fixed abode'.

Despite Nancy's protestations, I had originally wanted to produce a book for this walk but unfortunately the upheaval involved in moving house from Heslington to Flamborough, then settling in to the new house and finally having the loft completely converted proved too much work for me to devote the time to another publication. However, Nancy put the walk on to our website and also included the 'Tales' that I had collected from various friends as well as strangers along the way. These can still be read in that format but what I have done is to select a few of them and included them in this present book. A couple of them have already appeared earlier and you can find others at the end of this Episode. Inevitably, I have had to leave out literally dozens of stories. Please do not feel offended if yours is not included. Hopefully the selection that I have made will give a flavour of the great time we had during the five months we were walking.

One friend deserves special thanks and that is Alistair Lawson, my old running buddy from Loughborough days. Al entered enthusiastically into the spirit of our adventure and, as well as providing several Tales of his own, managed to cajole a number of his Scottish friends to tell their stories as well. I hope I'm not being too suspicious but I have sometimes wondered whether Al was hoping to use his good offices as leverage in trying to persuade me to finish off running the Pennine Way that we never completed in 1970. I still get reminders from him over 50 years later!

LEJOG background

For walkers, one of the exciting challenges of LEJOG (or the End to End Walk) is deciding which particular route to choose because there is all manner of possible variations. According to some experts, the shortest possible LEJOG waking route, entirely on roads, is 868 miles. But we opted to stay off road whenever feasible. Devising your own route, of course, means that there is no official distance for LEJOG. We wanted a route that would take us in a meandering line through or near to Oxford, Leicester, York and Whitley Bay in order that we could visit our four offspring along the way. This meant our planned route would measure a little over 1,200 miles and would take us through our new home at Flamborough.

Coincidentally, by Flamborough Lighthouse there is a toposcope with a map showing that the distance from Flamborough Head to Land's End is exactly the same (362 miles) as the distance to John o'Groats. In other words, Flamborough is the mid-point between the two ends of Britain 'as the crow flies'. This is assuming that crows always fly in straight lines and that they would wish to do a spectacular dog-leg journey via Flamborough in order to get from one end of the country to the other. So the fact that Flamborough would be half way (as the crooked crow flew) confirmed to us that it had to be along our route.

What later made this plan even more astonishing was that after I had carefully mapped out the chosen route for our 1,280 miles journey, with all its twists and turns and deviations and diversions, we discovered that Flamborough Head was in fact only half a mile away from the mid-point of our painstakingly measured distance! Just a slight manipulation of the route was sufficient to make it our exact mid-point position. An inebriated crow, accompanying us on our walk and meandering from side to side of the straight line direction, would therefore still be exactly half-way through the trek when it reached Flamborough.

We had agreed that Nancy would do all the teccy stuff – photos, computer, blog, emails and so on and I would be responsible for collecting the Tales. By the end of the walk I had collected 80 stories.

Shortly before she retired from Heslington, the Church put on a wonderful combined Centenary Birthday Party for Nancy (60 years old) together with her Methodist colleague Rory (40 years old). As preparation for our LEJOG walk, they gave her a lovely gift of a Rambling Rector climbing rose bush, alluding, I hope, to her love of walking and not, I trust, to the character of her sermons. It is now gloriously established in our new home.

Completing LEJOG is for some people a race against time and the record was reckoned to be held by a soldier of the Royal Artillery who in 1986 had completed the walk in just over 12 days. We planned to do it rather more leisurely; in fact, a lot more leisurely as we would be walking around 10-13 miles a day and so allowing ourselves some five months to finish the whole walk. You can see the line we followed on the accompanying map and **Appendix 1** describes the route in more detail.

The Christian Aid project to which we committed ourselves was a partnership project in Sierra Leone. This small West African state is about the same size and has about the same population as Scotland. It had suffered a brutal civil war in 2002 and was classed as one of the poorest countries on earth, being ranked as 180 out of 182 nations according to the UN Human Development Index.

The partnership project aimed to improve farming and to provide clean water in two parts of the country. What made the programme important was the fact that for every £1 that we raised for Christian Aid, the European Union would match-fund with another £3.50 – certainly a very attractive proposition to potential donors.

We had set ourselves a target of raising £10,000 and by the end of the venture we had collected £15,000. When this was match-funded, another £50,000 of EU money was added to the total, giving an overall figure of £65,000. We were, to say the least, delighted with the generosity of so many supporters and well pleased with the result.

LEJOG had been an exceptionally enjoyable venture. As well as reaching our financial target, we had met some wonderful people, had seen some fascinating places, had enjoyed great weather and there were almost no problems along the way.

One incident which could have ended in catastrophe but from which we emerged unscathed happened in Berwick and is related in the Lockpicker's Tale below. Perhaps reaching the Scottish border had made us a little over-confident and careless because we made the most foolish of errors. Yet the way we were rescued made us feel that we were being guided and protected even if we had been foolhardy. Here is the story.

The Lock-Picker's Tale by John Wakenshaw

It was 8.05 on Tuesday morning and I heard a call from over the garden wall: *'Hello, anyone there?'*

'Aye,' I replied.

'We're in trouble – we've locked ourselves out of the house and we don't know where the spare key is kept! And we haven't even got the owner's phone number or address with us – they're locked inside as well!'

So I went round and suggested that I might be able to help.

My job is doing home maintenance and repairs and I've sometimes had customers come to me and say that they have lost their house keys and they wondered if I could help them. Until recently I had to say 'Sorry, I can't'. So I decided that perhaps I should see if I could learn something about the noble art of lock-picking in order to help people who found themselves locked out of their homes.

I discovered that if you Google 'Lock Pick Tools' you can access scores of sites that give you all the advice that I needed. I was away! There are firms offering catalogues with details for all the gear you can use for lock-picking as well as for all the different sorts of locks: padlocks, safe locks, door locks. There is even a tool for getting inside letter boxes – you push the implement through the box and then twist it round to reach the key and then – hey presto – you just open the door! Anyone can learn the basic rules of lock-picking by just going on the internet.

I have now 'manufactured' my own set of lock-picking tools. This consists of a flattened Allen key and two picks made from the metal part of an old car windscreen wiper blade. It sounds like Heath Robinson but that's all you need.

The principle of picking a Yale type of lock, which is the kind that was giving Nancy and John their problem, is fairly basic. The cylinder of the lock contains five or six holes with five or six small pins (or plungers) of different lengths that fit into the holes. To open the lock, I had to put the lock pick into the cylinder and, one by one, push up the different pins. The Allen key is required to put 'tension' on the lock by holding the pins out of the way once they have been pushed up. It's important to apply just the correct amount of pressure and getting this right takes a bit of practice.

I've actually managed to open a Yale-type lock, using this method, in only 45 seconds. However, Nancy and John's lock was more tricky; the first five pins moved easily but the last one was more awkward. I was reasonably confident that I could do it but it demanded some patience. Eventually the pick did its work, the lock was released and the door opened.

What I had not said to Nancy and John before I started work on their lock was that I had only begun learning the techniques of lock-picking about two months ago. Although I had done a good bit of practice on dummy locks, I had not, so far, done a lock-picking job for real. So when I heard the cry from over the garden wall, I thought 'Ah! Here's the chance to put my skills to the test!' I suspect that Nancy thought I was an accomplished emergency expert but their lock was the very first one I've freed in a real situation.

I've still got a lot to learn. One ambition I have is to be able to cut new keys for people who have old locks but have lost the original keys. However, I'll not be learning how to use the 'bumper keys' that some official authorities fire from a kind of gun when they want to break through a lock and enter a building quickly in an emergency. And I don't intend to copy some Americans who do lock-picking as a hobby (on dark winter nights, perhaps?) to see who can crack the hardest lock in the shortest record time.

Oh, I nearly forgot. Once I'd set Nancy and John on their way for their day's walk, I went home for my breakfast and then went out to do my proper job – house repairs and maintenance.

Another story from the blog relates to our Wedding Anniversary on 29th July.

Bob Bagot is a good friend from my Waterloo Grammar School days. He had a copy of our walking schedule and had taken the trouble to go up to Scotland to meet us and then join us for a day's walk. But there had been no pre-arranged rendezvous. He just jumped out from the side of the road near Loch Lomond to greet us. I got the shock of my life! I persuaded him to write us a Tale. Here it is.

What a way to spend your Anniversary by Bob Bagot

Bob Bagot

Being bitten by midges, stumbling over rocks and tree roots, getting soaked (Probably. It is, after all Scotland), but fortunately not getting blistered by a heat wave (It is, after all Scotland). This was the choice for John and Nancy, celebrating their wedding anniversary on July 29th as they walked (epically) along the banks of Loch Lomond. I should say the 'bonnie banks' as it was a nice day. I know. I was there. Actually I was there 39 years ago when they got married but that part of the tale comes later.

I had decided to go to Scotland to climb a Munro and, having learned of their itinerary and timetable from their website, I thought I would try and coincide with part of their trek from Land's End to John o'Groats. So I am driving along the road from Drymen to Balmaha wondering whether they have taken the hilly route or the trudge along the road. Then I see this pensioner couple walking slowly but steadily just ahead. It is of course John and Nancy. I park the car ahead and wait. When they come past I get out of the car and say something inane like 'You do meet some strange people in the most unlikely places'. John looks up and thinks 'Oh no, not a confrontation with an obvious idiot!' He tentatively says 'Yes?' I say nothing. We go back over 50 years to when we were at school together so why should he recognise me in the middle of nowhere. Then recognition dawned. 'BOB!' he shouts in amazement. I love these surprise meetings. They were pleased and somewhat relieved it was not an obvious idiot.

We agreed to meet up again the next day, their wedding anniversary, and I was able to walk with them for an hour or so. We swapped news, family happenings, medical updates and sorted out the world's problems. It was great to meet Nancy again because I have only seen her once before, and that was 39 years ago. As I said earlier, I was at their wedding (was I an usher? – I can't remember). But why should I remember their anniversary after all these years? Well, it's because I got married the day after, so if I can remember my own ... (I usually forget but my wife has a habit of reminding me).

Actually, going to John and Nancy's wedding caused a great deal of aggravation for me. My wife's parents (at the time they were still – just – my fiancé's parents) were not too sure of the new man in their daughter's life. Was he from the wrong side of the tracks? It was a bit late for changes but they arranged a garden party the day before our wedding so that they could show off the 'new man' to all their friends and see how he behaved. Well, the garden party happened, but not the test for the 'new man' because he (i.e., me) wasn't there. I had gone to Eck's wedding. Now I definitely was from the wrong side of the tracks. But it all worked out in the end. We got married the next day and lived happily ever after. So did John and Nancy despite doing strange things on their anniversary. Next year is number 40 – Ruby – expensive – and I shall probably go back to forgetting their anniversary. But no doubt my wife will not let me forget ours.

I said above that we had had almost no problems on the walk. However, there were two that I should mention. The first was the fact that Nancy broke a small bone in her ankle when we were in Edinburgh and with many miles still to go before reaching John o'Groats. Was it a stress fracture? We cannot be sure but she did not realise that it had fractured and so continued with the walk, bearing the inconvenience with womanly stoicism. Perhaps it was just as well that we did not know it was broken or we might have had to think about the possibility of abandoning, or at least delaying, the rest of the walk.

The other problem related to myself. Completing LEJOG had been a great achievement but throughout the walk I had had one nagging disappointment – and the Scrabble Graph that Phil Hassall had faithfully updated each week on our blog says it all! Nancy had consistently stayed ahead through the five months gruelling competition and I would have to settle for the Silver Medal.

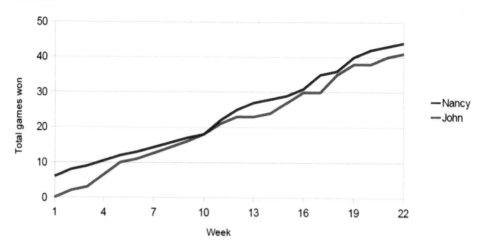

Do you think this might mean the end of our Scrabble playing days? You must be joking!

Throughout this walk, and our future ones, we received excellent support and encouragement from Steph Cooper, our Christian Aid line manager back at base in Yorkshire.

EPISODE 11
Other Long Sponsored Walks

I had continued my running during our stay at Heslington but sadly, when we returned from five months walking LEJOG, with no chance of running during that time, I just found I could not get back to anything like the (slow) speed I had been running before. Reluctantly, I had to call it a day. But running, track, road, country and fells, had been part of my life since I first started at Waterloo Grammar as an 11-year old in 1954 and the sport had given me enormous enjoyment. I could not complain. Now walking with Nancy became of even greater importance than it had been before.

After we completed **LEJOG** in 2011, we still continued doing long sponsored walks but, apart from **Walking St Hilda's Way**, there were no more books. Instead, we put information about the new walks onto our website **(www.johneckersley.wordpress.com)** and this Episode gives a summary of those walks.

2013 Carlisle to Bridlington (including Priory 900)

This was our first long walk designed specifically as a pilgrimage walk.

Bridlington Priory was founded in 1113 by Walter de Gant for Augustinian canons and is one of the earliest such houses in England. In 2013 Bridlington Priory would be celebrating the 900th year of its foundation and we were approached to see if we were interested in developing a pilgrimage walk as part of the celebrations. Naturally(!) we agreed and produced a linear walk, not inter-connected circles on this occasion, from York Minster to Bridlington and Nancy produced the accompanying booklet that gave route directions.

However, we found, almost by chance, that Carlisle Cathedral was also an Augustinian foundation and that it, too, was celebrating its 900th anniversary the same year. On top of that, a re-built Hexham Abbey, another Augustinian foundation, was also 900 years old. It seemed that we had to join all three centres into the one walk. So we agreed that Nancy and I would walk from Carlisle, along Hadrian's Wall, then across to Hexham before coming down through Durham to York where we would join the Bridlington Priory 900 walkers going on to Bridlington. Our idea was to pray in each of the churches that were open along our route; if they were closed, we would leave a greetings card.

Yet it might so easily got off to an embarrassing start. We had told Carlisle Cathedral beforehand that we were doing a sponsored Pilgrimage walk to raise awareness and money for a Christian Aid project for Women's Empowerment in Afghanistan. However, it was pouring down with rain on the Sunday morning that we were due to travel to Carlisle – it was a long journey and we wondered if it was really worth the trouble. Thankfully, conscience got the better of us and we arrived at the Cathedral just as the choir and clergy were about to process in. We looked at the weekly pew news-sheet – there it gave a special welcome to John and Nancy Eckersley, two pilgrim walkers who were going to be present in the service. We were included in the prayers and the youth group were looking forward to meeting us after the service. In the end, everything was fine but it had been a close call.

Thereafter, things went more smoothly. We had some heart-warming welcomes at the churches we visited. By the time we had reached Bridlington, the number of pilgrims had greatly increased and Nancy preached at the evening Communion service.

Captain Matthew Webb

2014 Dover to Carlisle

This was only about half the length of LEJOG but still extremely satisfying. Once again, we were favoured with lovely weather (the serious flooding in southern England had just about cleared when we started) and we met many inspiring people. We managed to raise over £6,000 for the same Christian Aid project in Afghanistan that we had supported the year before. As with LEJOG this was match-funded, this time 3:1, by the European Union so our figure became £24,000. We had made it a condition of the walk that we would pray in each of the eleven Cathedrals and Abbeys that we visited along the route.

There was no question as to where our start would be in Dover: it had to be on the seafront from the bust-statue of Captain Matthew Webb, the first person to swim the English

Channel. The reason for this is that Nancy found out a few years ago that she is distantly related to the famous pioneer; in fact she is Captain Webb's great-great-niece.

The first leg of the walk, from Dover to London, was pretty hectic. We passed no less than five of England's 17 UNESCO World Heritage Sites: Canterbury Cathedral, Maritime Greenwich, the Tower of London, Westminster Palace with Westminster Abbey and St Margaret's Church, and the Royal Botanical Gardens, at Kew.

Cathedrals and Abbeys that we visited, in addition to Canterbury and Westminster, were Rochester, Southwark and St Paul's. As well as calling at the Cathedrals, we made sure to go to some of the secular iconic sites: the London Eye, the Houses of Parliament, Downing Street and Lambeth Palace.

After London there was a number of places that we particularly wanted to visit and one of these was the Swinford Toll Bridge. This lies across the River Thames between the small settlement of Swinford and Eynsham, where once again we were staying with Roger and his family.

To reach Eynsham we had to cross the Thames at the Toll Bridge. The historic ford at Eynsham had always been dangerous but to build a bridge required considerable money. However, in order to persuade the Earl of Abingdon to foot the bill, a special Act of Parliament was passed in 1767 that eventually allowed the go-ahead and gave the ownership of the Bridge and its tolls to the Earl and 'his heirs and assigns **for ever**'. Moreover, the tolls were to be tax-free – the idea of income tax had not been invented – and the Bridge today remains a mini tax haven, free from income tax, capital gains tax, inheritance tax or VAT!

Pedestrians, pedal cycles and motorcycles are exempt from payment but other classes of traffic remain subject to tolls, which are 5p in the case of cars. Almost four million vehicles a year cross the bridge – that is, on average, a staggering total of 10,000 vehicles every day. This gives an annual income to the owner of some £200,000 – and they do not have to pay any tax on the revenue.

Depending on your point of view, this could be described as utterly insane in the 21st century. Others might describe its maintenance as a wonderful example of anachronistic British eccentricity.

In any case, walkers like ourselves have to be very restrained and not chortle smugly as we overtake the lines of frustrated drivers, waiting their turn to pay their 5p toll.

At Oxford, we turned roughly north-west and walked to the two villages of Lower and Upper Slaughter. We had wanted to visit the Slaughters partly because of their intriguing names but also because Upper Slaughter (though not Lower Slaughter) is a 'Thankful Village'.

The idea of a 'Thankful Village' was first suggested by Arthur Mee, the writer and journalist best known for his Children's Encyclopaedia. He had noticed that almost every settlement in the country had its own war memorial, commemorating those who had given their lives in the First World War. Very few places did not have a memorial. That fortunate few he called 'Thankful Villages' because they had lost none of their men in the 1914-18 carnage in which a million British lives were lost.

By 2013 a Wikipedia up-date had identified 53 'Thankful Villages' in England and Wales. Of these, a very small number (13) have come to be known as 'Doubly Thankful' because, as well as coming unscathed from the First World War, they lost no-one in the Second World War either. Upper Slaughter is one such Doubly Thankful village. Its name is clearly highly ironic.

Subdued, but at the same time hugely thankful for our own good fortune, we continued on our way. From the Slaughters we carried on over the Cotswolds and, crossing the Vale of Evesham, it was not far to Tewkesbury where we would turn north and follow the Severn Valley (all the way to Shrewsbury).

Tewkesbury Abbey, Worcester Cathedral and Shrewsbury Abbey each gave us very warm welcomes (we were getting used to this by now) as we continued north through Cheshire and into Lancashire. The next part of the route was probably the least scenically attractive of the whole walk, although it is full of interesting history and an important attraction we did not want to miss was Wigan Pier on the Leeds-Liverpool Canal.

People have for long joked about the idea of an inland industrial town like Wigan possessing a 'pier' – surely these are only found at seaside holiday resorts. Well, Wigan may not be a major holiday resort but it does have a pier – at least of sorts.

Wigan Pier

The original 'pier' at Wigan was a coal loading staithe, probably a wooden jetty, where coal wagons from the Lancashire coalfield were brought on a narrow gauge tramway to 'tipple' (unload) their cargoes directly into waiting barges on the adjacent canal. The original pier is believed to have been demolished in 1929 and the iron from the tippler sold as scrap. Today a replica tippler, consisting of two curved metal rails, has been erected at the original location.

In 1937, Wigan was featured in the title of George Orwell's book 'The Road to Wigan Pier' which dealt, in large part, with the desperate living conditions of England's working poor. Today, the dreadful environment he described has been reclaimed and ironically, Orwell's grim picture brought the town to public attention and is now an important marketing tool in encouraging the town's tourist potential.

Believe it or not, there were more canals and rivers to follow. From Preston, it was the Lancaster Canal towpath for much of the way up to Kendal. However, as we went through Lancaster, we did a slight detour in the town because we wanted to be able to say we had been to the centre of the Country.

Geography teachers (and quiz masters) delight in arguing about where the precise centre of our country is located. It largely depends on what geographic unit we are considering and on how we do our calculations. 'Britain' (or 'Great Britain') is the big island consisting of the three separate countries of England, Scotland and Wales. The UK ('United Kingdom of Great Britain and Northern Ireland') is those three countries plus Northern Ireland. And do we decide to include all our offshore islands or are we content to consider only the mainland? Different places have long jealously guarded their own claims to be the real centre of our nation.

There are two main ways of calculating the 'centre' – it can either be what is called the 'centroid' of the two-dimensional shape of the country or it can be the point furthest away from the sea. The two methods give quite different answers.

In 2002 the Ordnance Survey decided to settle the matter and conducted studies to determine impartially where the true centres of our nation and its constituent countries are to be found. They used the 'centroid' method of calculation. Simply speaking the centroid is the point at which a two-dimensional cardboard cut-out of the area could be perfectly balanced on the tip of a pencil. Offshore islands are assumed to be part of the area and to be attached to the mainland in their precise positions by invisible, rigid, weightless wires. This is a simplified way of visualising centroids; in practice the OS used a precise mathematical procedure.

The OS research came to the following conclusions:

(a) the centroid of mainland Great Britain (excluding islands) lies near Whalley in Lancashire

(b) when the islands are included the centroid is outside Dunsop Bridge in Lancashire.

However, for the purposes of our walk from Dover to Carlisle, the most interesting finding is the fact that the centroid for the whole of the United Kingdom lies near the junction of Fenham Carr Lane and Wyresdale Road (SD 49014 60926), about a mile south-east of Lancaster and close to the

Ashton Memorial. It was an easy deviation for us to make in order to claim we had been to the centre of the civilised world (and note: it was in Lancashire; not Yorkshire!)

The final leg of the walk used parts of the Miller's Way to Penrith from where the Eden valley led to Carlisle and our final Cathedral visit.

2016 Firth to Firth

Our main walk of 2016 was another sponsored effort for Christian Aid, again match-funded 3:1 by the European Union. Nancy has a dream of completing a circuit of the whole British coast. We finished England and Wales some years ago but the Scottish coast is a different kettle of fish and I'm highly dubious as to whether we will ever complete it or not. However, nothing ventured, nothing gained, so we opted for a 250 miles 'Firth to Firth' walk from Dundee (on the Firth of Tay) to Inverness (on the Moray Firth). Dundee is home to that great comic character, Desperate Dan.

Friends have often been envious, in a nice way, of the fact that we always seem to have fine weather on our treks, even when elsewhere in the country conditions have been dreadful. This time, though, our good fortune ran out. Four days of strong northerly winds and associated rain reminded us of how blessed we've been in the past. Probably the worst day was a 10-mile hike along a deserted beach when we saw not a single other person and had seven rain-swollen streams to cross. However, the good days were great. We're now able to boast how we've eaten Arbroath Smokies and Cullen Skink – amazing

Desperate Dan

how clever marketing can succeed in selling ordinary stuff as if it were caviar instead of fish soup.

Cullen Skink
The stuff in the bowl, I mean! (Nancy)

But the most bizarre incident happened just south of Lossiemouth, where there is an army firing range that shoots ordnance over the beach and out to sea. We had just started off along the path when we looked back and saw a long line of teenagers clearly doing the same walk as ourselves. They were from Gordonstoun School. Half a mile further on was a soldier on guard duty. The army was actually having a firing practice – we could hear it. Apparently, it seems that the military knew nothing of the School's walk but, thankfully, when the sentry saw the trail of students, he radioed his commander and the army immediately cancelled its practice. We wonder, did anyone ever bother to do Risk Assessments when Prince Charles was at Gordonstoun?

When we reached Inverness, we had now completed the whole of the east coast of Scotland. However, a quick glance at an atlas will show that any attempt at walking the west side of Scotland would be much more problematic.

2017 Coastliner Way

In 2015 we had completed our own 'Coast to Coast Walk' from Liverpool to Flamborough (see Episode 12). For the second half of the walk, from Leeds to the east coast, our route ran roughly parallel to the route taken by the Coastliner bus and we used that bus each day to get back to our parked car. The thought crossed our minds that the route we had taken from Leeds to the coast could, with just a little tweaking, be made into a Long Distance Walk.

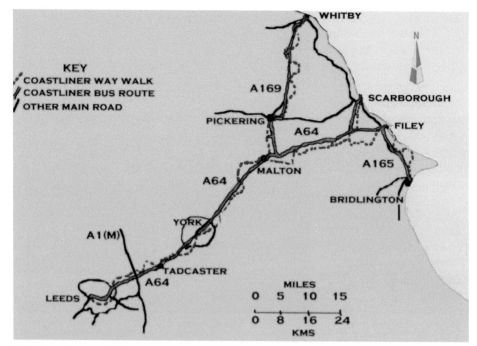

That's what we did and we called the walk 'Coastliner Way'. The attraction of the Walk is that each leg starts and finishes at a Coastliner bus stop. This means that, apart from getting to the start of a walk, there is no need to use private transport.

As far as the route itself is concerned, you first walk from Leeds to Malton. From there, three separate branches, corresponding to the 840, 843 and 845 Coastliner buses, lead to Whitby, Scarborough and Filey/Bridlington respectively, giving walkers a choice of routes to the coast. Total distances (including the three separate branches) add up to about 170 miles.

Unlike our previously devised walks, we did not publish Coastliner Way as a printed guide book. Instead, with great help from Phil Hassall, we put the walk on to our website and walkers can print out details of the different legs of the walk from the website. Although the route descriptions and maps are technically free to print, we asked users to make a voluntary donation to Christian Aid.

We inaugurated the Way with the customary sponsorship for Christian Aid.

2018 York Minster Pilgrimage

York Minster's Great East Window is the largest expanse of medieval stained glass in the country, a masterpiece in glass and stone depicting the beginning and end of all things. For 12 years the 600-year-old window had been the subject of a major restoration and conservation project – one of the largest of its kind in Europe. In May, for the first time in a decade, the restored window would be finally complete.

All 311 stained glass panels were removed from the 15th-century window, which is the size of a tennis court, in 2008 so York Glaziers Trust could begin the mammoth task of restoring the fragile masterpiece.

The project, which also involved the conservation or replacement of nearly 2,500 stones by York Minster's stonemasons, was part of the cathedral's £15m York Minster Revealed project, which ran from 2011 to 2016. The project has involved the installation of state-of-the-art UV resistant protective glazing, which was the first time the material had been used in the UK and the largest worldwide use to date.

We felt such a momentous achievement merited recognition and so we persuaded the Minster to support a number of Christian Aid Pilgrimages to add to the publicity. We ourselves followed the Coastliner route but this time going in the opposite direction, i.e., from Filey to York (approximately 62 miles) while other pilgrims took their own routes. The accompanying newspaper photo shows some of us at the conclusion of what was another very enjoyable walk. Although we did not know it at the time, this would be the last of our major sponsored walks.

Arrival at York Minster   *Courtesy David Harrison*

EPISODE 12
Round Britain's Coast and other Walks

As well as completing all the sponsored charity walks that we have devised and already described, I should point out that Nancy and I were doing lots of other walks, 'in our spare time' as you might say, whenever we had a holiday. We were especially interested in five kinds of walk:

(a) the official National Trails administered by Natural England

(b) other long walks recognised by the LDWA

(c) walks around the coasts of different islands

(d) devising our own Coast to Coast route

(e) and walking around the whole coast of Britain.

There is a list of all those we completed in the Appendix that we have compiled.

In **2017** we were counting up the number of **National Trails** we had finished and then, almost by accident, we found that the LDWA awarded certificates to walkers who complete a certain number of National Trails (there are currently 21 altogether). To obtain a Gold Certificate you have to walk 15 of these and, counting up our record, we realised that we had already done 14 and so there was only one left for us to do. I, of course, maintained a stiff upper lip suggesting how childish it seemed for a pair of old pensioners to be bothered about getting a couple of cardboard certificates. Nancy was having none of that; she was absolutely exhilarated by the prospect of 'Going for Gold'. And so it was. We walked the Pennine Bridleway in three bites and were thoroughly pleased with the trail.

Island Coastal Trails have included Anglesey, Arran, four of the Channel Islands, Isle of Man, Isle of Wight and Lindisfarne.

2015 saw us create our own Coast to Coast Walk which we called 'All our Yesterdays'.

Pilgrimage has received a great boost in respectability in recent years and 'making a pilgrimage' (religious/spiritual or secular) is a good way to explore the countryside as well as to recharge the batteries.

Although it is not a pilgrimage walk, many people have been inspired by Alfred Wainwright's Coast to Coast Walk from St Bees Head to Robin Hood's Bay but there are many other alternative itineraries that link Britain's east and west coasts. In fact, AW encouraged walkers to seek out their own routes. That is what we chose to do for this venture as we had already done Wainwright's walk, as well as others including David Maughan's North of England Way.

We were conscious that there was a number of friends we had not seen for many years, even though we had been sending them regular Christmas greetings. Perhaps we ought to make a point of seeing them before either they or ourselves died. So we devised what we called a 'Thanksgiving Pilgrimage', linking together places that have been important to each of us throughout our lives. At each location we would meet some of the many people in those places that had been positive influences in our lives, especially family members, school teachers and Church leaders. Hopefully, there would also be opportunities to reflect on how we might be spending the rest of our lives.

It was relatively easy to construct a linear route across the country. I was born in Liverpool; Nancy and I met and married in Manchester; Nancy had been born in West Yorkshire; we spent most of our married life in York and we have now retired to Flamborough on the East Yorkshire coast. Conveniently this route can be classed as a 'Coast to Coast' walk (from Irish Sea to North Sea) and the boot-dipping-in-the-water ceremony had to be a compulsory part of the venture.

Starting in Liverpool we followed the first part of the Leeds-Liverpool Canal (I had never realised that this started in Leeds Street, Liverpool and finished at Liverpool Street in Leeds). This, like so many other canals, has been transformed since I was a youngster. Even near the city centre we spotted a heron.

Approaching Waterloo along the Canal, we noted, not surprisingly, that the foul-smelling leather tanning works which were a feature on my school cross-country runs have long since disappeared. And the field where I used to play football has now been lost beneath the giant container terminal attached to Seaforth Dock.

Christ Church, Waterloo, the huge sandstone building which was such an important part of my childhood, but which could not be maintained by its declining congregation, has been put in the care of the Churches Conservation Trust. It is now used for, amongst other things, farmers' markets and beer festivals. Thankfully, the fine Grade 2 listed building has been saved from demolition and the congregation has been able to transform the parish hall into a new 'church' and this building is far more manageable and easier to maintain. We saw encouraging evidence of new growth at my cousin John's church – the people there meet in a converted cinema – and we met friends from my Church and Scouting days, including Brian, who had only months to live. There was also the opportunity to visit my Mother's grave in Thornton.

Walking from Liverpool to Prestwich in north Manchester is not high on most ramblers 'must-do' lists so plotting a route was challenging. However, crossing the 'Carrot Country' of West Lancashire brought back memories of potato and pea picking as a teenager, although I never aspired to carrot collection. Perhaps the memories of that hard labour (and very poor pay) have influenced my sympathies for workers who are so often exploited in our world today.

On reaching Prestwich we went to the Church where we had been married and renewed the vows we had made 43 years earlier. This church had also seen major changes. An arsonist had set the place on fire in the 1970s and that had necessitated major alterations to the interior. The building is now considerably more 'modern' and accessible and we mused on the way that good can sometimes come from ill. In Lancashire we met Dennis and Margaret, the couple who introduced me to the glorious excitement of fell running, and then called to see Kathy and Gordon, Nancy's School (I nearly said 'old') French teacher and her husband. We were reminded that with good friendships, conversations can be resumed decades on with barely the suggestion of any break in time. I wonder: is eternity going to be like that?

Crossing the Pennines, the weather was glorious and the views far-reaching. But having left industrial Lancashire we soon came to the industrial West Riding. Dewsbury, Nancy's birthplace, was our next target. The streets and houses of her earliest days were still very much the same and so too was the church where she had been baptised as a baby.

Leaving the Calder Valley we made our way around the south-east of Leeds using parts of the Leeds Country Way. This is a circular walk around the city and whilst some parts are very attractive, it's difficult to devise a satisfactory way across the network of motorways converging on the city. Nevertheless we managed it and came out at the edge of the Rhubarb Triangle, Yorkshire's answer perhaps to West Lancashire's 'Carrot Country'. Since 2010 'Yorkshire Forced Rhubarb' has been given official European Commission 'Protected Designation of Origin' status. Yorkshire folk, apparently, are immensely proud of this recognition but, coming from the other side of the Pennines, I just smile indulgently. Whilst in the West Riding we made sure to look up Roy, one of Nancy's cousins and Graham, the teacher I worked with as a VSO in the Sudan nearly 50 years before.

From Tadcaster to York, the easiest walking route is the Ebor Way, a direct line following the way of an old Roman road across the Vale of York but this does involve walking over a pedestrian crossing on the main line East Coast railway. Calling at York Cemetery to visit the site of my Dad's ashes, who should we meet, totally unarranged, but Sharon and Stuart.

Since getting married, York had been our base until Nancy retired in 2011 and so this was where we were expecting to meet most people. The Minster, where Nancy had been ordained, was an obvious place we had to visit. So, too, were the four churches with which we had been first associated. All four appeared to be thriving and they looked inviting with attractive notice boards, well-kept, colourful front gardens and a buzz of activity. Nancy, of course, was delighted that the church-community centre that she had helped to plant is virtually fully booked for all manner of community events.

When we came to Heslington, the church welcomed us back with open arms. So did the primary school where I took assemblies. And I was delighted that neither community had forgotten my weakness for chocolate cake!

For the penultimate part of our pilgrimage we followed the Yorkshire Wolds Way, the National Trail that runs along the crest of the chalk escarpment. We had walked this trail numerous times in the past and so it was a different sort of pilgrimage; not so much meeting up with old friends and church congregations but rather being refreshed by long-remembered beautiful scenery. We were blessed indeed; anticyclonic conditions over the whole of the UK ensured delightful, warm, sunny weather on the hills even if the morning mists still lingered over the Vale of Pickering below us.

Of course we had to call in to see Nancy's mum, Barbara, and sister, Kathy, when we reached Filey and we paid our respects at the site of Nancy's Dad's ashes in Filey churchyard.

The walk finished along the Yorkshire coast as we took the beach along Filey Bay and then the cliff path past the internationally important RSPB site at Bempton, round to the magnificent clifftop at Flamborough Head and then finally down to dip our boots in the North Sea, just half a mile from our home in Church Close.

What had we learned?

We'd had time to reflect and to give thanks for the important influences of so many different people in our lives. We were constantly reminded of how blessed we have been with good health and the freedom to walk in such a wonderful country. Oh yes, and it was good to learn that we were not yet quite past it. What's next we wondered?

Completing the Walk around the Coasts of England, Wales and Scotland

Over the last few years we have been using every holiday opportunity to nibble away at our long-term project of walking the whole of the British coast and we completed doing England and Wales in 2004 with a glorious September week in Sussex. The whole of the trek so far had covered approximately 3,000 miles. It had been enormous fun and Nancy celebrated on the last day with her first successful attempt at water-skiing. Unfortunately, I couldn't join because I was required to stay on the boat and take the photos ... the reader must surely understand.

However Scotland, with its highly indented coastline, would be an entirely different matter. Nancy was undeterred and so in recent years we have been doing different sections of Scotland's seaboard.

At this point I must tell you first about **Magnesian Limestone**. It is a rock outcrop which runs in an almost continuous belt from Nottingham on the River Trent to South Shields on the River Tyne – that's roughly 260 miles.

I've been intrigued by the concept of Magnesian Limestone ever since I was at Durham studying Geography over 50 years ago and, after the Head of the Department had taken us all on a half day 'field trip' to a nearby Mag Lime quarry at the beginning of the three-year course, he casually told us we had to present him with an essay with a title something like 'Write all you know about Mag Lime'. We weren't given any suggested reading list and there was no internet browsing in those days. I hadn't a clue where to start! Every so often I've had flashbacks to that traumatic assignment. But it's been a love-hate relationship really because, secretly, I've had a yen to know more about the stuff and in 2016 I started looking into the idea of creating a long distance walk along the rock outcrop.

Planning the route went well and in the beginning of 2019 I asked Mark Comer to do the printing for me.

Then in April I was diagnosed with leukaemia. My increasing tiredness meant that long walks were no longer feasible. It will sound very strange for me to relate what happened next but, to my astonishment, I felt in one way a certain sense of relief. I say this because throughout the preparation I had been experiencing bouts of niggling uneasiness, as if something was not quite right. I have already mentioned on a number of occasions how God's Spirit, God's Guidance or however you prefer to describe the Inner Silent Voice has been a major factor in my life. For me, this was further proof that all our ways are under his control. So when the diagnosis came, I realised that this had been a forewarning from God that the Magnesian Limestone Way Trail was not to be.

As I was no longer able to walk more than a few miles a day, it also meant we had to alter our plans for finishing walking the Scottish Coast. Therefore in summer (2019), instead of us both doing the walk, I drove the car and acted as support for Nancy, stopping every few miles along the route to make sure she was all right, and she was able to walk without having to worry about how she would get back to the start of the day's trek. I have to say that it worked extremely well; I was not at all frustrated and it gave us both the opportunity to see, for the first time in our lives, the stunning majesty of North-West Scotland.

There is now only about 250 miles (five weeks walking) left to do. If my health does not deteriorate too much in 2020 I'll do the supporting again and Nancy should complete her dream.

On every long walking holiday Nancy and I have been on for the last ten years or so we have said to each other, 'This may be the last walk we ever do – you can never tell what might happen' and so we have treasured each time as if it were the last. But they have gone on and on and we have been constantly reminded how blessed we have been.

Conclusion

There is one difficult question that I feel I must address. Some of you reading this summary of my life may be thinking: 'That's all right for you, John, but it's never happened like that for me. And how can you ignore the suffering – mental, physical, emotional and financial – that so many people have to go through and whose lives have never been anything like 'filled with the fullness' that you have described?' I offer a couple of thoughts for your consideration.

I can only tell you what has been true for my own life. Yes, there have been occasional difficult times but these have been trivial compared to other people's problems. I feel that if I were not to write as I have done, it would be selfish of me not to share the fullness of life that God has given to Nancy and myself. Don't misunderstand: I'm not in any way whatsoever boasting about my experiences of God's Spirit but, on the other hand, to ignore those times would be to exclude the major driving force of my life and to give a quite unbalanced picture of who I am.

In the New Testament we read of how the early Christians felt moved by the Holy Spirit to do this or that, or to go here or there. There is sometimes a danger of assuming that such motivations do not happen any longer today. But they certainly do and if you read books like 'That Other Voice (in search of a God who speaks)' by Graham Turner – I came across the book earlier this year – you will see what I mean.

Towards the end of Nancy's walk in Scotland earlier this year, she felt moved to go into St Bride's Church in North Ballachulish – the only church she visited apart from those where we worshipped on Sundays. On the bookstall was a copy of 'In the Midst of Life' by Jennifer Worth, the author of 'Call the Midwife'. In her 'Last Thoughts' at the end of the book, Jennifer wrote in 2011 how, only six months after her book was first published, she was diagnosed with cancer of the oesophagus and with secondary cancers in her bones. Yet she wanted her readers to know that she was completely at ease with the diagnosis. 'I have no fears, no worries, no regrets,' she wrote, 'I do not try to struggle against this – I accept it as part of life ... as everything slips away what I am left with is faith and love ... Thanks be to God.' I feel this conclusion of Jennifer's closely matches my own feelings as I approach 'Life in all its Fullness', beyond what we traditionally call Death.

I said in my Introduction how Jesus' promise to his listeners that 'I have come so that you will have Life, Life in all its fullness' has been of great importance to me. Nancy and I have had such lives – full of God's rich blessings. We wish you the same.

• • •

Postscript: *Since I wrote the above in December 2019, my latest visit to the hospital has confirmed that my blood levels have remained stable. If they continue to do so, Nancy may yet see her dream fulfilled.*

APPENDIX 1
LEJOG Route Description

SECTION 1 · Land's End to Glastonbury

We set off from the Land's End Hotel where, the night before, we had been invited to an amazing banquet, including oysters, smoked salmon, lobster, dressed salmon, tomato and basil salad and all kinds of sweets and cheeses together with sparkling rose wine and cocktails including a Land's End Sunset. All this was being held to celebrate the refurbishment of the Hotel. Was this a good omen?

It seemed so. The first sponsorship we received was from a young Manchester couple who, seeing our LEJOG tabards, drove their car up to their next roundabout, turned round and came back to offer us a donation. And they had never even heard of Christian Aid.

The South West Coast Path, half of which we would be following, is Britain's longest National Trail. There are plenty of ups and downs and according to one person's calculation the full route includes climbs totalling 114,931 feet (35,031 metres) which is nearly four times the height of Everest. Thankfully, we were only doing half of it.

The Cornwall and West Devon Mining Landscape (Poldark country) is a UNESCO World Heritage Site but the old mine shafts, chimneys and spoil heaps looked a bit grim in the mist and drizzle. Then, when the mist had cleared we suddenly met two old friends from Liverpool, Peter and Angela Stanley whom we had not seen since our wedding nearly forty years ago. This was to be the first of a number of unplanned, chance (?) meetings that we would have along the way.

From the end of the SWCP at Minehead, we struck inland across the Quantocks (we had never been to these lovely hills before) and then continued through Bridgwater to Glastonbury where June and Andrew, Tanya's in-laws, live. Of course we had to climb Glastonbury Tor. Coming down from the hill, we got chatting to some folk who had a distinct Geordie lilt in their talk. In fact, they told us that they came from Newbiggin-on-the-Sea. 'What a coincidence', we said. 'Our church organist, Peter Main and our good friend Joan Patton came from there'. Then it transpired that the lady we were conversing with had been their Sunday School teacher some 40 or 50 years previously. These chance meetings were starting to add up.

All the time along the way I had been collecting various Tales.

SECTION 2 · Glastonbury to Market Harborough

Carrying on to Wells and its fine Cathedral, we then crossed the limestone of the Mendip Hills and came to Bath. Bath marks the start of the Cotswold Way, which we had previously walked and we were reminded that the hilliest parts are right at the start of this trail. However, we soon left the hills and made north-east to join the Thames Path. We made a day detour to visit to the Roman town of Cirencester where we learned that the Cotswold Lion is the area's most famous breed of sheep.

We followed the Thames Path all the way to Eynsham, just outside Oxford, where Roger and Karen had offered us accommodation. At the edge of Oxford we turned north along the Oxford Canal and then came to the centre of Banbury. From here we took a rather twisting route, through Daventry to Market Harborough. This is where our daughter Tanya her family joined us and walked a short stretch with us – they gave us accommodation for the next few days at their home in nearby Leicester.

SECTION 3 · Market Harborough to Flamborough

We followed the Midshires Way and then the Macmillan Way to Oakham where we were mesmerised by the story of the Oakham horseshoes. Rutland, we noted from the wayside posters, is fiercely proud of its regained independence from the indignity of having been temporarily consumed by Leicestershire.

In Grantham we stayed bed and breakfast in a guest house only three or four doors down the road from where Margret Thatcher's father had his grocer's shop.

It was from here that we made a diversion to visit Woolsthorpe Manor where Sir Isaac Newton reputedly had his gravitational epiphany as he watched the apple falling from the garden tree.

Continuing north through Lincoln, we picked up the Viking Way as we followed the edge of the Lincolnshire Wolds to the Humber Estuary. We had not expected it but the Hull Churches had arranged a welcome party for us to escort us across the Humber Bridge into Yorkshire. On the other side of the estuary we turned east to go through Hull, across Holderness to Hornsea. This marked our break point.

Interlude

When we had started the walk we were literally 'of no fixed abode' because we had not yet completed the purchase of our new house in Flamborough. However, that had been settled while we had been on the trail and we now needed to transfer all our belongings from various locations and bring them to the new house. We did not stop walking completely but kept in fitness with just two days walking during each of the three weeks we were resting. Then we were off again.

SECTION 4 · Flamborough to Berwick

Picking up the trail again at Hornsea, we soon reached Flamborough and continued straight up the North Sea Coast. Navigationally, we knew this stretch of the route should have been easy – we had walked it numerous times before and there were always bus services to return us to the start of a day's walk. Along the way, various groups joined us. Sharon came from York with her daughter Leia and old friends from Heslington and new friends from Flamborough all provided excellent company.

Joining the Cleveland Way at Filey, we followed the cliff line to Saltburn. The prospect of crossing the River Tees at Middlesbrough did not sound attractive but we had a hilarious time going to and fro on the Transporter Bridge while the operator regaled us with his stories.

Since the closure of Durham's last coal mine, there has been an amazing transformation of the derelict former collieries and spoil heaps and the Durham Coast Path is today a fine, bracing walk.

Then, on Tyneside, we were met by our second son, Peter and his family. They again gave us accommodation and from there we had the delights of the Northumberland coast all the way up to Berwick. We had reached the Scottish border and were maybe becoming just a little over-confident. John Wakenshaw's Lockpicker's Tale is perhaps the most amazing of all the stories we collected.

SECTION 5 · Berwick to Fort William

This part of the Coastal path is part of Nortrail – the North Sea Coastal Path Project that aims to link footpaths and sites around the coasts of countries bordering the North Sea. It includes the John Muir Trail. John Muir was born in Dunbar and became one of the foremost conservation campaigners responsible for the establishment of the USA's National Parks.

Going across the Scottish Central Belt between Edinburgh and Glasgow, we made use of canal towpaths and then, leaving Glasgow, we made for Milngavie, which we had been warned is pronounced 'Mull-guy'. This is the start of the West Highland Way that runs for 95 miles to Fort William. It goes past some of Scotland's most majestic scenery including Loch Lomond, Ben Nevis and the Glencoe Pass. On this section we had another totally unexpected encounter – see Bob's Tale above.

SECTION 6 · Fort William to John o'Groats

From Fort William to Inverness we used the obvious line of the Great Glen Way that runs along the line of the Great Glen Fault, a geological gash separating the North West Highlands from the Grampians. Then for the last stretch of the walk we hugged the coast all the way up through Sutherland and Caithness to our journey's end where friends were waiting to greet us. Stuart and Brenda Turner from Heslington had specially arranged their Scottish holiday to coincide with our arrival at John o'Groats. They even provided us with a celebratory banquet of Cornish crackers, Wensleydale cheese and Scotch whisky!

APPENDIX 2
Nancy's theological reflection on Scrabble

In the Beginning was the Word – or rather a word, as words spelt with capital letters are not allowed. Scrabble begins with a single word. Nothing can happen until that single word is down – the pattern on the board cannot begin to be created without that first word.

In our experience, Scrabble is best played by two enfleshed human beings. The rules say it can also be played by three or four people, but we have found the best games are a 'Trinity' – him, me and the tiles on the board. The game does seem to have a life of its own. There are good boards and difficult boards. Boards which are open and those which seem closed up. Tiles which seem determined to clump together vowels or consonants and do not give the nice balance from which high-scoring words can be made. The tiles sometimes seem to be 'on my side' or 'against me'. Or, it could be viewed as a nature/nurture problem. The gift of good tiles, high scoring letters, opportunities to play the 'all-outers' against the more demanding skill needed to make something of a mediocre group of letters. The spirit can sometimes be willing – but the concentration is weak.

Scrabble can have its own ritual food. The bowl of crisps or nuts, the glass of wine or lager, can add to the experience of the interconnectedness of yourself with the game. And of course some have an experience of Scrabble which dates from childhood (like me) whilst others have an adult conversion to the game (like John).

We have found that there are different interpretations of the game of Scrabble:

1. There is the fundamentalist method of playing, where the stated rules on the lid of the box are the thing you have to go by. There is no deviation or interpretation allowed. These are the rules and so you must follow them or suffer the penalties. The dictionary (Chambers) is the judge and jury of

the permissibility of a word, careful attention being paid to its derivation. If the word is not permitted, then the tiles must be removed and a turn is forfeited. Once a blank is played, it remains on the table and always represents the letter for which it was originally played.

2. There is the liberal interpretation – the blank can be 'swapped' if you have that letter. The dictionary can be used as a check (before playing) or even, at the extreme liberal edge, opened and browsed through to try to find a suitable combination of letters that might fit (the Sea of Browsing you might call this). If a disallowed word is found to have been played then of course the player can have another try without penalty. There are also books of Scrabble words (no meanings). These can be consulted and no requirement is made of whether a player knows the meaning of a word or not.

3. There can also be the local language of the game. Here are three examples in Eckersley language:

   a. To 'Poxon' means to place all seven of your letters down on the board on your very last go in a game – thus snatching victory from the jaws of defeat as your opponent is left with their own letters to deduct from their final score. This is named after a certain John Poxon, a Methodist Minister with whom we played regularly in Jamaica. John played a solid game often deliberately and quietly falling behind his wife (and John and myself) as he played but then snatching the victory at the last minute in this way – it seemed every time we played!

   b. To play 'Scunthorpe'. This term was given to us by 'Auntie Edna' (who was in her 90's and a mean Scrabble player and crossword fanatic). She did not play this way herself but was forced to do so by someone else she played with. It means to play in a fundamentalist way (see above) in a mean and crabby way – if you cannot use an opening yourself you spoil it for your opponent.

   c. To have a 'Gentleman's'. This means if you have a lousy hand (all vowels or suchlike) and it is your turn, you can ask your opponent for a gentleman's agreement that both of you will throw your hands in and pick new tiles. Of course it reveals to your opponent that you have a poor hand – but it does mean that if they also have a weak hand and agree, the game is vastly improved.

But the end times (eschatology) of the contest can make or break what has gone before. It can be easy to lose concentration if your opponent (or partner in the creation of a game) is slow and you feel you are sufficiently far ahead to be out of reach. St Paul did keep his eyes fixed on the goal, running towards it; and there is the saying that 'It is not the beginning but the continuing of the same until it be thoroughly finished which yields the true glory!' Or, as we say in our household: 'No game's won until the final whistle'. Come to think of it, that might also be said of walking from Land's End to John o'Groats!

APPENDIX 3

LONG DISTANCE WALKS NANCY AND I HAVE COMPLETED TOGETHER (The LDWA defines a 'Long Walk' as being one of over 20 miles in length) Distances are mostly those given by the LDWA's digital measuring system.

Name	Miles
Knaresborough Round	20
*Land's End to John o'Groats	1,300 (by the time we had finished)
Leeds Country Way	62
Millennium Way (Isle of Man)	28
Minster Way (E Yorkshire)	50
*Nidd Valley Link	28
Nidderdale Way	54
**North Downs Way	125
**Offa's Dyke Path	177
**Peddar's Way & Norfolk Coast Path	133
**Pembrokeshire Coast Path	181
**Pennine Bridleway	205
*Rezzy Rush	40
**Ridgeway	85
Ripon Rowel	50
**South Downs Way	100
**South West Coast Path	630
*(Walking) St Hilda's Way	40
*St Hilda's Way reconnoitre	84
Tabular Hills Walk	48
**Thames Path	184
Thanet Coastal Path	20
Three Peaks Yorkshire	24
Tidewater Way	90
**West Highland Way	94
*Whitby Abbeylands Walk (circles)	132
Whitby Way	66
*Wilberforce Way (circles)	101
Yoredale Way	72
*York Minster Pilgrimage	62
**Yorkshire Wolds Way	79

Round Britain's Coast
(excluding sections already counted in the above table)

Our English Coast Path	2,027
Our Welsh Coast Path	757
Our Scottish Coast Path (as of 2019)	1,776

NOTES:

1. *Indicates routes we have created ourselves (some of these are not included in the LDWA list because there is no written publication for them). The mileages given for those that are made up of inter-connected circular walks are the totals for all the circular routes.

2. **Indicates National Trails

3. I have excluded a good number of walks that overlapped with other routes we were walking but which were not entirely completed.